DIMENSION: LANGUAGE '94

CHANGING IMAGES IN FOREIGN LANGUAGES

June K. Phillips
Jeffrey L. Buller
Gladys C. Lipton
Flore Zéphir
Audrey L. Heining-Boynton
David B. Heining-Boynton
David C. Alley
Clara Krug

Robert M. Terry
Editor

Selected Proceedings of the 1994 Joint Conference of the
Southern Conference on Language Teaching
and the
Foreign Language Association of Georgia

© 1994 by the Southern Conference on Language Teaching
Valdosta State University
Valdosta, Georgia 31698

Library of Congress Catalogue Number: 94-67409
ISBN 1-883640-02-4

CONTENTS

Review and Acceptance Procedures
SCOLT *Dimension*

The procedures through which articles are reviewed and accepted for publication in the proceedings volume of the Southern Conference on Language Teaching (SCOLT) actually begin with the submission of a proposal, including an abstract, to present a session at a SCOLT Annual Meeting. Once the proposal is received, it is read by members of the Program Committee.

Once a session has been accepted, the presenter(s) is(are) contacted by the Editor and invited to submit an article for consideration for publication in *Dimension*, the annual volume of conference proceedings. Upon notification of interest, copies of the publication guidelines are sent to the presenter(s). Prospective authors submit four copies of the manuscript. The articles are then sent, with the title page containing the authors' names and affiliations removed, to the nationally prominent SCOLT Editorial Board, and each article is reviewed by at least three of these specialists. Normally, articles are sent to reviewers who have expertise in the area treated by the article. The reviewers are asked to make one of three recommendations: (1) publish as is; (2) publish after rewriting; or (3) do not publish.

Once these recommendations are received by the Editor, he reads each article and makes the final decision whether or not to publish it. As a result of these procedures, at least three individuals decide whether or not to include the oral presentation in the Annual Meeting, and then four different people read and approve the article before it is selected to appear in *Dimension*.

Introduction

"Changing Images in Foreign Languages"—this was the theme of SCOLT's 1994 Annual Conference that again met in conjunction with the Foreign Language Association of Georgia (FLAG). This past year the role of foreign languages has begun to change. With the passage of Goals 2000, we are now seen as part of the core curriculum in American schools. The work on national standards has contributed to the unification of the profession. Foreign language education will surely change as a result. Change is healthy; it signifies vitality and evolution.

The articles that appear in this year's volume of *Dimension: Language '94* were selected from among the presentations given at this year's Annual Meeting. The first article is written by June K. Phillips, our keynote speaker in Atlanta, and is based on her speech. "The Challenge of Setting National Standards for the Study of Foreign Languages" addresses the work of the Task Force for foreign languages, a group of educators charged with developing a set of draft standards for American students learning another language. There are many far-reaching implications of this work on national standards, one of which is competency-based assessment. There will be changes—changes not only in the teaching of foreign languages but in the preparation of teachers, changes in how we determine what students should know and be able to do, and changes in our view of just how good is good enough. The insight provided by June Phillips is first-hand; she is the Standards Project Director.

Jeffrey L. Buller's article, "Cicero's *Pro Caelio*: Text and Context," addresses the inclusion of Cicero as an optional part of the College Board's Advanced Placement course in Latin literature. As Buller points out, this is the first time since 1973 that any Latin prose author has been included in the course as an option. Its inclusion, however, will truly pose formidable challenges for Latin teachers: the teachers' lack of familiarity with the text; the challenging vocabulary and grammar of the text; its relationship to a group of poems by Catalase, and the novelty of this being the first occurrence of Cicero's work on this test with no track record of practice. Buller, therefore, offers suggestions for each of these areas to Latin teachers and recommends a character study, a sociological study, or a rhetorical study as a focus for a successful AP course in Latin literature.

In "The Basic Components of FLES*: Communication and Culture," Gladys C. Lipton explains the different types of FLES* (foreign languages in the elementary school) programs—sequential FLES, FLEX, and Immersion. Note: The asterisk indicates this term as the "umbrella" for all types of elementary school foreign language programs in grades K-8. Lipton points out several reasons why anyone should even consider offering FLES* courses. She discusses why communication is the first basic concept of FLES*, stressing the use of "native language kid talk" (NLKT) in classroom activities. Finally, She emphasizes the role of culture, especially what she calls "people-to-people culture," relating classroom cultural content to the students' interests in day-to-day activities.

Flore Zéphir, in "Multiculturalism in Elementary French Textbooks," has examined thirteen current first-year college French textbooks in order to address the issue of the extent to which textbooks contribute to the promotion of multiculturalism. She explains the term "multiculturalism" as "the study of various cultures outside the dominant society or traditional mainstream." This obviously includes ethnolinguistic minorities within the countries where the target languages being studied are spoken. Zéphir sets forth three basic categories of multicultural coverage as a result of her research: (1) limiting francophone coverage to "facts-only;" (2) limiting this coverage to the reading skill alone; and (3) the insufficiency of multicultural activities. She then offers suggestions for integrating multiculturalism through active language use and activities.

The article, "Learning Styles, Personality, and the Foreign Language Teacher," by Audrey L. Heining-Boynton and David B. Heining-Boynton, deals with learning styles in the foreign language classroom, more specifically, the types of "teaching styles" exhibited by foreign language educators. The authors question if there is, in fact, a correlation between these teaching styles and the learning styles that teachers themselves exhibit. In describing the learner, the authors include a discussion of personality type indicators, such as the Meyers-Briggs Types Indicator. Their study is based on data gathered from a group of 78 female and 5 male teachers. They attempt to discover if there is a predominant learning/teaching style among foreign language educators, if these educators exhibit a predominant personality type, and the implications that these typings have for foreign language students.

The final article in this 1994 volume of *Dimension* is "Other Voices: Afro-Hispanic and Francophone Literature," written by David C. Alley and Clara Krug. This article specifically addresses one of the strong changes in education in general, including foreign language education—a change away from the more traditional "academic canon that systematically focused on the accomplishments of Europeans while ignoring those of other ethnic groups." As the authors state, this change in focus "attempts to teach all students the values of tolerance and respect for diversity." Alley and Krug then address practical questions related to identifying techniques for teaching culture, developing new instructional materials, and integrating these materials into the existing curriculum. They offer samples of two Afro-Hispanic texts and two francophone texts, along with sample activities.

Change is truly abounding in foreign language education—national standards, multiculturalism, the resurgence of FLES*, the consideration now given to learning styles, the "new" role of Latin literature in Advanced Placement courses and tests for Latin, all of which are addressed in this annual volume of Dimension. There is an old saying—"Stability in a language is synonymous with rigor mortis." Languages change because they are living. Language education should, therefore, embrace change so that it can reflect this vitality. The articles in this current volume clearly show the "Changing Images in Foreign Languages."

Acknowledgements

The Southern Conference on Language Teaching (SCOLT) would like to recognize the commitment of Valdosta State University in supporting the work of the organization and foreign language education. I would especially like to thank Lee Bradley, SCOLT's Executive Director, for his dedicated work on this and previous volumes of *Dimension*.

Without the willing assistance of the SCOLT Editorial Board, this volume would not see light. Their promptness in returning manuscripts, their thoroughness in reading first drafts and in offering suggestions to authors, and their willingness to serve on the Editorial Board cannot go unnoticed and unappreciated. It is through their work, coupled with the high-quality articles that are submitted for publication, that *Dimension* has become recognized as a major publication in the field of foreign language education.

—Robert M. Terry
Editor

Board of Directors
Southern Conference on Language Teaching
February 1993-February 1994

1

The Challenge of Setting National Standards for the Study of Foreign Languages[1]

June K. Phillips
Weber State University

The political and educational agendas in our country are reverberating with the dynamic of change and the desire for reform. Professional changes have confronted second language educators for a number of years in the struggle with a paradigm shift that has challenged conventional thinking about the goals and objectives of language instruction as well as how it is learned. Broader purposes for language study and a growing research base in second language acquisition have led to instructional approaches that emphasize the developmental aspect of language learning rather than a mastery model; envisioning the student as an interactive and creative learner has led to richer content through authentic documents and to a more process-centered approach within the expressive modalities.

The most momentous change has evolved from global concerns that recognize the importance of second languages in the curriculum and from the pressures that will follow national standards and competency-based assessment. Many of our institutions, both precollegiate and in higher education, have already embraced initiatives that have charged the profession to describe communicative performances in terms of some useful and usable level of proficiency. Even "teaching for the test" has taken on a wholly new role in recognition that performance measures legitimize that linkage, i.e., teaching to an accepted criterion. Fortunately, stronger research and evolving theories of second language acquisition enrich instructional practice.

As teachers strive to translate more fully communicative approaches into classroom instruction, along comes educational reform with its emphasis on content standards and new assessments. In Washington and in state capitols, two questions dominate discussion of education:

- What should students *know* and be able to *do*?
- How good is good enough?

The search for answers to these questions has resulted in a governmental focus on the creation of content standards—knowing and doing, and performance standards—how good in a number of academic disciplines. At the beginning, the very real fear existed that foreign languages would be ignored in the process. Fear of being left out has shifted to the challenge of being included. (For background on the National Educational Goals Panel and the inclusion of foreign languages in the federally funded standards project, see Phillips and Draper, 1994.)

Standards and Changing Teacher and Learner Roles

The Task Force[2] charged with developing a draft set of standards for U. S. students learning world languages share their work regularly with the profession and incorporate appropriate suggestions. Undoubtedly, the document will be amended many times before its public implementation. Even at this early stage, however, standards setting entails a number of daunting challenges that will shape the image of the foreign language education profession, and the roles teachers and students will have to assume if these "world class" standards to which the government aspires are to be achieved.

In the current draft, the standards address five focus areas for students. First and foremost, the standards seek to have students *communicate across cultures*. This standard builds upon the proficiency orientation and functional approach to language learning of the last decade. It underscores, however, an integrative view of language and culture. For teachers, this standard implies that as individuals we will have to strive for the greatest possible degree of proficiency in the target language and competence in observing, analyzing, and reflecting upon the target culture. Note therein the challenge to higher education: at the preservice level, the development of the nation's future teachers will require a whole new cooperative effort between departments of foreign languages and pedagogical specialists. It will also render extended study abroad a necessity rather than a luxury. In a world where classrooms will be replete with unedited and unglossed magazines and books from target cultures and where television broadcasts will beam in everything from music videos to interactive student discussions on global issues, the teachers' language proficiencies must be strong enough so that they have the confidence, the comfort, the credibility to provide access to those materials for their students. Colleges and universities will have to revamp curriculum to promote these proficiencies. It is not acceptable to have a freshman enter the university from a strong high school program with an intermediate-mid on a proficiency test and exit having achieved only an intermediate-high rating in speaking, a timid standard for certification whether set by states or by institutions.

Another focus areas of the draft standards will be that of a strong *knowledge and experiential formation in the target cultures* that encompasses life styles, literary expressions, traditions, and artifacts of target cultures. Study of a society's language should expand appreciation of its culture in ways that a disciplinary monolingual focus cannot achieve. Avoidance of the stereotypes and disconnected trivia too often part of today's classes will occur when the teaching force has benefitted from extensive time in country and from preparatory courses that approach cultural studies from an anthropological perspective.

A key draft standard focus is that of enabling students to *acquire new information in a second language,* information or a perspective that would not have been available to them had they not acquired a new language and effective strategies for learning. After all, that is the primary reason for everything else. Our hopes rest in a new generation of students capable of reading and of listening to world events, to creative works, to entertainment that enriches an otherwise parochial monolingual existence that their global peers will have transcended. Our hopes rest in a generation able to speak to and write to one another without the limitations imposed by one-sided translations. These goals also require that the profession expand its vision of the content of the foreign language classroom. Selections should not be grounded solely in teacher choice but in areas of student interest. This does not imply that foreign language teachers need also to be geographers or political scientists, art historians or sports reporters. It does mean that developing a more broadly based interdisciplinary focus that serves as a model for our students will enable second language courses to become more powerful in their content.

Standards are also being proposed for enabling students to *participate more fully in their communities and in the global marketplace* by using second languages here at home and abroad. The old cliche about foreign languages having no practical use for students in middle America or anywhere else no longer holds up. Regardless of region, or economic or social class, today's students have ample opportunities to interact with speakers of languages other than English. Moreover, their social and career aspirations require them to do so.

Finally, the standards will attempt to address the unique cognitive and affective outcomes that foreign language study brings to those who pursue longer sequences. Chief among the advantages, albeit a longer range outcome, is that of *gaining insight into one's own language and culture* by dint of having studied a second one. This may be challenging to specify in measurable terms, but an effort will be made to render explicit and outcome that most serious second language learners have sensed.

Teachers for the New Standards

The reality is that the changes we are facing will be major for some teachers and programs, minor for others. An important dimension of all standards projects resides in the provision for professional development. Teachers must not become targets of reform but must assume the role of agents of reform. The challenge lies in the profession's managing change with a minimum of discomfort, but realistically one must be ready to tolerate a bit of ambiguity, take a few risks, think divergently—in essence think just as critically in our roles as teachers as we would want students to do in their roles as learners.

At this juncture in the profession, instructional change requires a totally new dimension of professional development as well as a revamping of teacher education programs. The day of "methods" and prescriptions and "cookbooks" of neat ideas has passed. When dealing with the spectrum of human communication, it no longer suffices to exert tight instructional control which carefully dispenses prescribed structures and vocabulary and formulaic messages. Learners must also be prepared to confront unique utterances and text. They must become adept at processes and not just products. The bottom line is **empowerment**. To empower learners, there must first be empowered teachers: teachers empowered to reflect on their classes, teachers empowered to observe learning and facilitate it, teachers empowered with strong proficiencies in the target languages so that they feel confident in using materials from a variety of sources and content areas. Teachers have long wanted to be decision makers; they now have the opportunity to be so; they also need the information upon which to base wise decisions. Inservice and preservice programs must prepare teachers to *think* and not to imitate sheepishly or follow strict formulas.

Effects of National Standards

The national standards project could succeed in changing how children and young adults learn second languages in this nation. To do so, the profession must agree to move forward with instruction and assessment that recognizes the value of foreign language study for a broad spectrum of learners. Teachers, too, will have to embrace the concept of lifelong learning for themselves so that they continue to expand their linguistic proficiencies, their knowledge of the cultures for which they hope students develop understandings, and the research base upon which viable instructional approaches are built.

Notes

1. A portion of this article is taken from the keynote address, "The Challenge of Change in Standards-Setting Times," delivered by June K. Phillips to the Southern Conference on Language Teaching in Atlanta, February 1994.

2. The Task Force charged with writing the standards is chaired by Christine Brown (Glastonbury Public Schools, CT). Members are: Martha Abbott (Fairfax Public Schools, VA), Keith Cothrun (Las Cruces High School, NM), Beverly Harris-Schenz (University of Pittsburgh), Denise B. Mesa (Dade County Public Schools, FL), Genelle Morain (The University of Georgia), Marjorie Tussing (California State University at Fullerton), Guadalupe Valdes (Stanford University), John Webb (Hunter College High School, NY), and Thomas E. Welch (Kentucky Department of Education).

Reference

Phillips, June K. and Jamie B. Draper. "National Standards and Assessment: What Does It Mean for the Study of Second Languages in the Schools?" in Gale K. Crouse, Ed. *Meeting New Challenges in the Foreign Language Classroom.* Report of the Central States Conference on the Teaching of Foreign Languages. Lincolnwood, IL: National Textbook Company, 1994.

2
Cicero's *Pro Caelio*: Text and Context

Jeffrey L. Buller
Georgia Southern University

In 56 B.C., a Roman by the name of L. Sempronius Atratinus—only seventeen years old at the time—brought formal charges against M. Caelius Rufus, then in his mid-twenties. Caelius was accused of violating the Lex Lutatia de vi, proposed in 78 B.C. by the consul Q. Lutatius Catulus. Enacted at a time when the civil strife between the supporters of Marius and Sulla was of recent memory, the Lex Lutatia outlawed "violence of a political nature" including such revolutionary acts as taking up arms against the Senate, attacking civic magistrates, and attempting to undermine the government.[1] In point of fact, Caelius was not accused of any of these things. He was implicated in a murder, the poisoning of the academic philosopher Dio. What made Dio's murder a political act, according to Atratinus, was that the philosopher had been serving as an ambassador in Rome at the time of his assassination.[2] The "political violence" attributed to Caelius consisted, therefore, of financing Dio's murder by borrowing money from Clodia, one of three daughters of Ap. Claudius Pulcher. Atratinus also charged that Caelius had then attempted to murder Clodia, too, in an effort to conceal his crime.

As was common in Roman courts, the charges brought by Atratinus included other accusations, not all of them strictly related to the case. Working with fellow prosecutors, P. Clodius[3] and L. Herennius Balbus, Atratinus accused Caelius of mistreating his father, earning the contempt of his fellow townsmen, sexual immorality, association with the conspirator L. Sergius Catiline, extravagance, and participating in a riot that occurred as the Alexandrians were escorting Dio to Rome. The case came to trial in early April. On the third day of that month, in an open court of the Forum Romanum, the three prosecutors presented their case. The following day happened to be a holiday, the Ludi Megalenses, on which theatrical entertainments were performed at the Temple of the Magna Mater on the Palatine Hill. Ordinarily, trials would have been suspended for the duration of this festival. But since the Lex Lutatia had been enacted to deal with crimes of the greatest severity, it permitted no holiday to be taken. On April 4, 56 B.C., therefore, in the only trial conducted that day in the entire city of Rome, the defense of Caelius was presented. Caelius himself spoke first. The triumvir M. Licinius Crassus spoke second. Speaking third and climactically was a former consul who had been one of Caelius' own teachers.

The case of M. Caelius Rufus would probably be of only limited historical interest were it not for the fact that the third person to speak that day was the famous Roman orator M. Tullius Cicero and the speech that he delivered the *Pro Caelio*. The *Pro Caelio* is a remarkable document in every sense of the term. It presents a dramatic and highly complex legal argument. It contains references to, and at times scandalous revelations about, some of the most famous figures of the late Roman Republic. And it makes its defense of Caelius, not by dealing directly with the substance of the accusations, but by redirecting the entire focus of the case. To high school teachers of Latin, the *Pro Caelio* is also important for another reason: beginning in 1994, this speech will be an optional part of the College Board's Advanced Placement course in Latin Literature.

Allowing teachers to include the *Pro Caelio* as part of the AP course is a major innovation. It represents the first time since 1973 that any Latin prose author has been included in the course as an option. Moreover, the *Pro Caelio* is a text that confronts teachers with a number of formidable challenges:

- Most high school teachers have never taught this work before and they are unlikely to be familiar with it;

- Both its vocabulary and grammar are significantly more challenging than the works of Cicero usually studied at the secondary level (the *Catilinarians*, the *Pro Archia*, and the speech *On the Manilian Law*);

- The College Board's syllabus of the Advanced Placement course is designed in such a way that the *Pro Caelio* cannot be read in isolation but must be studied in combination with a group of poems by Catullus;

- At least for several years, there will be no "track record" for the test; teachers will not have earlier versions of the exam that their students may take as a "trial run."

In light of all these obstacles, why did the College Board choose the *Pro Caelio* as the sole prose option in the current AP syllabus? The answer to this question is that this speech has a number of qualities that make it ideally suited to the course. More than any other speech of Cicero, the *Pro Caelio* lends itself to sharing a syllabus with the poems of Catullus. It deals with the same segment of society and refers to many of the same individuals who are mentioned in Catullus' poetry. In addition, it has the advantage of *not* having been widely taught in high school Latin courses: unlike the *Catilinarians*, the *Verrines* and the *Philippics*, passages from the *Pro Caelio* are rarely excerpted for introductory and intermediate Latin texts. Students who encounter the *Pro Caelio* in the AP course will thus be studying it without any preconceived notions. Finally, the structure of the *Pro Caelio* has both similarities to and differences from the structure of a "typical" Ciceronian oration: for this reason, students who are already familiar with the progression *Exordium/Narratio/Partitio/Argumentatio/Peroratio* will be able to locate these elements in the *Pro Caelio* but perhaps not always at that point in the speech where they expect them.

In this way, the *Pro Caelio* has the potential of providing a valuable alternative to the traditional Advanced Placement course based on the works of Catullus and Horace alone. Nevertheless, in order for teachers to present this new course successfully, they will need to know which resources will help both themselves and their students improve their understanding of this speech, how it might be possible to integrate the *Pro Caelio* into a syllabus that also includes works of poetry, and which pedagogical approaches might be adopted so as to provide a coherent picture, not only of Ciceronian oratory, but of late Republican literature as a whole. Because of the importance of these issues, it will be best to deal with each of them in turn.

The New Advanced Placement Syllabus
and Recommended Resources

The first resource that any teacher will wish to obtain before planning the new course in Cicero and Catullus is the current year's Advanced Placement Course Description for Latin Literature (College Board).[4] The AP course description includes a wealth of useful information, including a listing of those passages that students must master before taking the exam. For example, the booklet makes it clear that, while it is beneficial, it is not necessary for students to read every word of the *Pro Caelio* in Latin. The AP exam will cover only sections 1-9 (Cicero's introduction to the speech and his defense of Caelius' character), 30-50 (Cicero's counterattack against the character and motives of Clodia), and 79-80 (Cicero's peroration).

Nevertheless, while it is possible to understand the *Pro Caelio* after reading only these three sections, there are certain drawbacks to doing so. The three recommended portions of the speech do contain nearly all of the work's most famous passages, avoid the more repetitive sections of the work, and provide a reasonably cohesive summary of the work's major arguments. Students whose sole exposure to Cicero has been the *Catilinarians* will find the *Pro Caelio* quite challenging even in an edited form. On the other hand, the speech contains very little that is not germane to Cicero's central thesis. Thus, if students fail to read sections 10-29, they will miss an important passage where the orator refutes the charge that Caelius had been a close associate of Catiline. If they omit sections 51-78, they will fail to see how Cicero deals with the central issues of the case. They may even get the false impression that the orator never bothers to address these matters.

For this reason, each teacher will need to decide for each individual AP course whether the advantages of teaching the entire speech compensate for the significant investment of time that this requires. At issue are the students' abilities in reading extended passages of difficult Latin and their need to spend additional time improving their skills in writing extemporaneous essays. In most courses, the best solution may be as follows: even though sections 10-29 are not on the exam, reading them in Latin adds continuity by allowing the students to read the first fifty sections of the speech in their entirety; sections 51-78 may be skipped, if time requires, but they should be read in English and thoroughly discussed in class so that students will be familiar with the issues addressed in them.

Second only in importance to the College Board's course description is Walter Englert's *Bryn Mawr Commentary on the* Pro Caelio (Englert). This work contains a brief introduction to Cicero, a succinct historical account of the background to Caelius' trial, a short bibliography, a complete text in Latin, and (most importantly) more than fifty pages of notes dealing with every aspect of vocabulary, grammar, and history that a high school class is likely to need. Ideally, one copy of the commentary should be ordered for each student in the course. This may serve as their primary textbook. If funds are limited, there should be at least one copy always available in the classroom and on reserve in the school's library.[5]

The third resource that teachers will wish to have available is R.G. Austin's annotated edition of the *Pro Caelio*. Unlike the *Bryn Mawr Commentary*, Austin's work is likely to be more valuable to the teachers themselves than to their students. A thorough introduction, copious notes, and several appendices provide useful information but probably at too advanced a level for most students. Teachers, however, will find Austin's commentary invaluable in preparing their own work for class and in choosing topics for discussions about the text.

Once the teacher has obtained copies of these three resources, it is time to consider the best way of organizing the Advanced Placement course. Which approaches should be adopted in order to integrate the *Pro Caelio* with Catullus' poems? How is it possible to teach such diverse authors as Cicero and Catullus in the same course while still providing some degree of continuity? Can the *Pro Caelio* be used as the basis for a broader analysis of Roman literary techniques or style? Certainly, different teachers will prefer to answer these questions in different ways. Nevertheless, as a first step, they might consider three major approaches to take towards teaching the *Pro Caelio*:

- The Character Study,
- The Sociological Study, and
- The Rhetorical Study.

Though not mutually exclusive, each of these approaches can provide a focal point for a successful AP course in Latin literature.

The Character Study

The "character study" is based upon the following premise. Both the *Pro Caelio* and the poems of Catullus refer to intriguing characters of the late Roman Republic. What do we learn about these characters from Cicero's speech and Catullus' poems? Is that information likely to be accurate? If these works were the "source materials" for writing a biography, would the biographer have enough information? What do Cicero and Catullus *not* tell the reader about these characters and why is this information missing?

Asking questions of this sort encourages students, not only to "mine" the Latin sources for biographical material, but also to consider how the modern world forms its impressions of historical or fictional characters. If, for instance, a class were to select a character from Roman literature such as Caesar or Pompey or Aeneas or Dido and list every adjective that came to mind when they thought of these figures, how could they explain where those impressions came from? They would probably find, much to their surprise, that they could not go back to specific texts and locate Latin words that were equivalent to most of the adjectives on their lists. A great deal of our impressions about characters comes from our "reading in between the lines." Performing an exercise of this type, therefore, helps students to realize how authors actually develop their characters. Moreover, it suggests that characterization often reveals more about the personality of the author than it does about the nature of the characters themselves.

This discovery is what makes the "character study" of Cicero and Catullus so fascinating. Which characters are mentioned repeatedly by each author? What does the reader learn about them? *How* is that information conveyed? Are the impressions that one receives about these characters consistent or do they vary according to the author's personality and intentions.

One obvious candidate for an exercise of this kind is the figure of Clodia, the sister of Cicero's nemesis, P. Clodius Pulcher. Clodia, at least if one accepts her traditional association with Catullus' "Lesbia," is discussed extensively in both the poetry and prose of the AP course. As a result, she provides the perfect "linchpin" between the two halves of the syllabus. Best of all, however, she is a fascinating figure in her own right. Clodia was born early in the first century B.C. Nearly an exact contemporary of the poet Lucretius, she was about ten years younger than Cicero, five years younger than Caesar, and seven years *older* than

Catullus. Her husband, Q. Caecilius Metellus Celer, died three years before the date of the *Pro Caelio*. Suspicion, but no evidence, suggested that Clodia had had Metellus poisoned. She began an affair with Caelius shortly thereafter. It is the animosity resulting from the end of this relationship that Cicero blames for the current case. Clodia was still living in 45 or 44 B.C., as may be seen in Cicero's references to her in his letters to Atticus (see, for instance, *Ad Atticum* 12.42 and 12.47). But the orator stops speaking about Clodia soon after and she must have died at about this time.

These then are the facts that can be known about Clodia's life. But what can be determined about her *character*? If one looks only at the text of the *Pro Caelio*, this is the image of Clodia that emerges:

SECTION	PASSAGE	TRANSLATION
18	*hanc Palatinam Medeam*	this Medea of the Palatine
31	*muliere non solum nobili verum etiam nota*	a woman not only noble but also notorious
32	*cum istius mulieris viro—fratrem volui dicere; semper hic erro*	with this woman's husband—I mean brother; I always make that mistake
35	*Tu, vero mulier—iam enim ipse tecum nulla persona introducta loquor—si ea quae facis, quae dicis, quae insimulas, quae moliris, quae arguis, probare cogitas, rationem tantae familiaritatis, tantae consuetudinis, tantae coniunctionis reddas atque exponas necesse est. Accusatores quidem libidines, amores, adulteria, Baias, actas, convivia, comissationes, cantus, symphonias, navigia iactant idemque significant nihil se te invita dicere.*	Now, as for you, woman—yes, I'm going to speak to you now as you really are and not playing one of your "roles"—if you expect to justify your actions, your words, your charges, your efforts, and your accusations, you'll also have to give us a full explanation of your relationship with Caelius, your "friendship" with him, your intimacy with him. The prosecution has been bandying about words like "debaucheries," "affairs," "adulteries," "trips to Baiae," "trysts on the beach," "parties," "revelry," "music," "concerts," "cruises" . . . and they imply that they do none of this without your approval.

36   *qui te amat plurimum, qui propter* [Your brother, Clodius,] loved
nescio quam, credo, timiditatem you very much. I suppose it was
et nocturnos quosdam inanis because of some—oh, I don't
metus tecum semper pusio cum know—fear of the dark or
maiore sorore cubitabat. something that when he was a
little boy he always used to
crawl in bed with you, his older
sister.

38   *Nihil iam in istam mulierem dico;* Now, of course, I'm not saying
sed, si esset aliqua dissimilis istius anything at all about *this*
quae se omnibus pervolgaret, quae woman. But if there *were* some-
haberet palam decretum semper one — not at all like Clodia,
aliquem, cuius in hortos, domum, you understand, but *someone*
Baias iure suo libidines omnium —who gave herself to everyone
commearent, quae etiam aleret she met, who obviously always
adulescentis et parsimoniam had her eye on someone, in
patrum suis sumptibus sustineret; whose gardens, home, and
si vidua libere, proterva petulan- cabana at Baiae an army of
ter, dives effuse, libidinosa sleazy gigolos felt right at home,
meretricio more viveret, adul- who supported throngs of young
terum ego putarem si quis hanc men and supplemented their
paulo liberius salutasset? meager allowance by paying
them for their services ... if
there were a widow who lived
however she wished, a shame-
less widow who lived scandal-
ously, a rich widow who lived
opulently, a promiscuous
widow who lived like a whore,
shouldn't regard a man who
was a bit loose in his treatment
of a woman like that as just
being "red-blooded"?

55   *Totum crimen profertur ex inimica,* This whole accusation (against
ex infami, ex crudeli, ex facine- Caelius) has originated in a
rosa, ex libidinosa domo. household that is destructive,
disgraceful, callous, depraved,
and indecent.

55   *temeraria, procax, irata mulier* lewd, impudent, vengeful
woman

62	*nisi forte mulier potens quadran-*	unless, perhaps, that resourceful
	taria illa permutatione familiaris	woman became an intimate of
	facta balneatori.	the bath-attendant through one
		of her two-bit transactions.

78	*eadem mulier cum suo coniuge et*	that woman with her
	fratre	brother-*cum*-boyfriend

After the class has encountered a group of passages such as this, the teacher may find it valuable assign an exercise similar to the following:

1. What is the image of Clodia that emerges from these passages? Underline specific words that Cicero uses to convey this impression.

2. What effect does Cicero achieve by his frequent use of the word mulier with reference to Clodia? Why does this word serve his purposes better than words like *femina, domina,* or *matrona*? (If the students have access to the *Oxford Latin Dictionary*, they should carefully examine the various connotations of each of these words.)

3. What effect does Cicero achieve by his frequent use of *ista* when referring to Clodia? How would the effect have been different if he had used *illa, haec,* or *ea*?

4. How does Cicero use sound to intensify the force of his words? Note specifically the presence of alliteration and other poetic devices.

5. What effect is achieved through Cicero's references to Baiae? (Baiae, a fashionable resort near Naples, was notorious for its opulence and the promiscuity of its clientele. In English, it is difficult to convey the same impression that Cicero creates with a single word. One creative exercise, therefore, might be to have the class name cities that a modern speaker might use to produce a similar effect. "Weekends in Las Vegas," "a fling in Acapulco," and "a hideaway in Cancún" are all possibilities.)

6. Does the intensity of Cicero's language suggest genuine moral indignation at Clodia's behavior or is the orator merely adopting a posture that will help his client?

After the students have completed this exercise—and, especially, after they have expressed their opinions about the last question—they may find it interesting to read section 29 of Plutarch's *Life of Cicero*. In this passage, Plutarch repeats an allegation that Cicero's wife, Terentia, not Cicero himself, had been responsible for the orator's poor relationship with Clodia's family. Terentia, Plutarch asserts, was jealous of Clodia because Terentia believed that she wanted to marry Cicero. Certainly, Plutarch (who dates to the late first and early second centuries A.D.) is writing long after the events that he is describing. There is little, if any, contemporary evidence to corroborate the story. Nevertheless, in a letter written precisely one month after the assassination of Julius Caesar (*Ad Atticum* 14.8), Cicero does ask his friend Atticus to tell him what has become of Clodia (*Clodia quid egerit, scribas ad me velim*). Moreover, Cicero spent the better part of a year attempting to buy the very same house and garden that, in the *Pro Caelio*, he had denigrated as the site of Clodia's numerous orgies.

Analyzing Clodia's character also provides the teacher with an excellent opportunity to incorporate direct comparisons between Cicero's text and the poems of Catullus. If the class has already completed its unit on Catullus, they might be asked which of his poems portray "Lesbia" in similar terms to those surrounding Clodia in the *Pro Caelio*. In most cases, one of the first poems that students will suggest will be Catullus' bitter denunciation of his former lover, poem 11:

> *Furi et Aureli, comites Catulli,*
> <u>*sive*</u> *in extremos penetrabit Indos,*
> *litus ut longe resonante Eoa*
>   *tunditur unda,*
> <u>*sive*</u> *in Hyrcanos Arabasve molles,*   5
> <u>*seu*</u> *Sagas sagittiferosve Parthos,*
> <u>*sive*</u> *quae septemgeminus colorat*
>   *aequora Nilus,*
> <u>*sive*</u> *trans altas gradietur Alpes,*
>   *Caesaris visens monimenta magni,*   10

> *Gallicum Rhenum horribile aequor ulti-*
> *mosque Britannos,*
> *omnia haec, quaecumque feret voluntas*
> *caelitum, temptare simul parati,*
> *pauca nuntiate meae puellae*   15
> *non bona dicta.*
> *cum suis vivat valeatque* moechis,
> *quos simul complexa tenet trecentos,*
> *nullum amans vere, sed* identidem *omnium*
> *ilia rumpens;*   20
> *nec meum respectet, ut ante, amorem,*
> *qui illius calpa cecidit velut prati*
> *ultimi flos, praetereunte postquam*
> *tactus aratro est.*

Reviewing this work, therefore, allows the teacher to ask many of the same questions about "Lesbia" that the students were asked about Clodia in the *Pro Caelio*.

1. What is the image of "Lesbia" that emerges in Catullus 11? Underline specific words that the poet uses to convey this impression. [Be sure to draw the students' attention to moechis ("adulterers") in line 17, *identidem* ("one after another") in line 19, and *ilia rumpens* ("bursting their loins") in line 20.]

2. What effect does Catullus achieve by referring to "Lesbia" as *meae puellae* in line 15? Why does Catullus use this term rather than *mulier* as Cicero had done in the *Pro Caelio*? (Remind the students that Catullus had used this expression affectionately in his earlier poems to "Lesbia," as in Catullus 2 and 3.)

3. How does Catullus use sound to intensify the force of his words? (Note specifically the alliteration of sive throughout the second quatrain and the force of such exotic words as *Indos*, *Eoa*, and *Hyrcanos Arabasve*.)

4. Does the intensity of Catullus' language suggest genuine moral indignation at "Lesbia's" behavior or is the poet merely suffering from a broken heart? Do you believe that, if Catullus had lived longer, he would have tried to win her back?

Once the class has completed this comparison between Clodia as she appears in the *Pro Caelio* and "Lesbia" as she appears in the poetry of Catullus, they should also be provided with a copy of Marilyn Skinner's sobering article on the "historical" Clodia (Skinner). Writing in a style that is easily accessible to most AP students, Skinner argues that *both* Cicero's and Catullus' portrayals of this characters are gross exaggerations, created for the authors' own rhetorical purposes. The *real* Clodia, Skinner argues, "is, alas, much more conventional. It is hard to think of her as the victim of unruly passions; she seems, on the contrary, firmly in control of her own life. Thus the Clodia of history turns out to be the direct antithesis of the Clodia of myth" (Skinner, 286-287). Why, the students might be asked, did both Cicero and Catullus distort the image of Clodia/"Lesbia" in their works? How does Skinner go about recreating a "true" image of this character? What does her conclusion tell us about the reliability of *other* characterizations in the works of these two authors?

As a means of continuing this comparison between the *Pro Caelio* and the poems of Catullus, teachers may want to have their students read Catullus 58 and 77. Neither poem is required on the College Board's syllabus[6] and the obscenity of poem 58 may make it inappropriate for certain schools. Nevertheless, because these poems do contain explicit references to Caelius, they make valuable companion pieces to the *Pro Caelio*. Poem 58 provides a graphic image of "Lesbia" that is fully compatible with Cicero's characterization of Clodia in the *Pro Caelio*. Poem 77 offers clear proof that Catullus regarded Caelius (whom Cicero would take such pains to portray as a modest and upstanding young man) as responsible for ruining his relationship with "Lesbia."

After reading these works, the students might be asked such questions as: How does the image of Caelius that appears in these poems correspond to his characterization in the *Pro Caelio*? What accounts for their similarity? What accounts for their differences? Are either of these images similar to the picture of Caelius that emerges in the fourteen letters written by Caelius to Cicero during the latter's governorship of Cilicia (*Ad Familiares* 8.1-14)? What may be learned from the two letters that Caelius wrote to Cicero during the events leading to Pompey's final break with Caesar (*Ad Familiares* 8.15-16)? If you were to write an article on the "historical" Caelius similar to Marilyn Skinner's article on the "historical" Clodia, how would you go about reconstructing a more complete understanding of this figure?

Finally, in courses where students have already read the *Catilinarians*, it is useful to contrast the image of L. Sergius Catiline that appears in *those* speeches to the image of this character that appears in the *Pro Caelio*. Why does Cicero take such pains in sections 9-14 of the *Pro Caelio* to demonstrate that Catiline, whom he still regards as having been responsible for the greatest possible threat to the Republic, as having had a number of good qualities? Why does Cicero say, in section 14, that he himself was almost taken in by Catiline's charm? An analysis of how Cicero characterizes Catiline in this speech helps to explain how this individual, who appears as such a scoundrel in the *Catilinarians*, could ever have been popular with certain elements of Roman society. Moreover, it illustrates just how far Cicero was willing to go in the interest of his clients.

The Sociological Study

A second major approach to the *Pro Caelio* is to examine the text for what it reveals about the society and values of the Romans during the late Republic. As anyone who has read the *Pro Caelio* realizes, this speech provides a fascinating "behind-the-scenes" glimpse into the beliefs and attitudes of the Roman aristocracy. When students are encouraged to view the *Pro Caelio* as a source of sociological material, they may be asked such questions as: What clues does this work offer us about the values shared by Caelius and his companions? Does this picture confirm or refute the image of the Romans that we derive from other authors of this period? Does Cicero seem to share Caelius' values or does he merely defend them as a way of protecting his client?

One way of beginning to answer these questions would be to set aside some class time during which the students are asked to translate (or retranslate) two passages selected from sections 34 and 40-41. In the first of these passages, Cicero imagines that a famous Roman of the "old school" is addressing Clodia.

> *Mulier, . . . ideone ego pacem Pyrrhi diremi ut tu amorum turpissimorum cotidie foedera ferires, ideo aquam adduxi ut ea tu inceste uterere, ideo viam munivi ut eam tu alienis viris comitata celebrares?*

> Woman, ... did I refuse to negotiate with Pyrrhus only so that you could daily strike bargains with your shameless lovers? Did I bring water to the city only to slake your lust? Did I build my road

only to provide a place for you to strut about, attended by the husbands of other women?

In the second passage, Cicero discusses the decline of morality that he believes to have occurred since the great days of the early Republic:

Verum haec genera virtutum non solum in moribus nostris sed vix iam in libris reperiuntur. Chartae quoque quae illam pristinam severitatem continebant obsoleverunt. . . . Itaque alii voluptatis causa omnia sapientes facere dixerunt, neque ab hac orationis turpitudine eruditi homines refugerunt; alii cum voluptate dignitatem coniungendam putaverunt, ut res maxime inter se repugnantis dicendi facultate coniungerent; illud unum derectum iter ad laudem cum labore qui probaverunt, prope soli iam in scholis sunt relicti.

But these sorts of virtues (i.e., the "old Roman virtues") are not only missing from our lives. They may scarcely even be found in our books. The very pages that tell us of old values such as honor and duty are left moldering on our shelves. ... There are even some scholars today who argue that everything should be done for the sake of pleasure. Yes, even supposedly learned people are no longer appalled by such an idea. Others believe that virtue can be *combined* with pleasure. Unbelievable! Simply by twisting a few words, they try to unite qualities that are wholly incompatible. Only one school still teaches that hard work is what leads a person down the narrow road to virtue. And they are left almost alone in their classrooms!

These two passages are particularly informative because they allow the teacher to move from a discussion of the *Pro Caelio* itself to the larger issues of Roman history, life, and society. For instance, after reading these passages, the students might be asked: Whom does Cicero imagine to be speaking in that first passage? (Even if they have never *heard* of Ap. Claudius Caecus, it should not be very hard for them to find out who this is. There were not many Romans, at least in the Republic, who built a road *and* an aqueduct ... even fewer of them who lived in the time of Pyrrhus of Epeirus.) How can Claudius be a relative of Clodia and what does this change in spelling reveal about a corresponding change in Roman values? (Which segment of Roman society was most likely to mispronounce "Claudius" as "Clodius"? Why might a person wish to flatter these people by adopting a substandard spelling of one's own name? How might earlier Romans have felt about this?) Also, after a brief discussion of the Epicureans, the Peripatetics, and the Stoics, the students should be able to identify the three different schools of philosophy to which Cicero is alluding in the second passage.

These two sections of the *Pro Caelio* also provide the teacher with an opportunity to address the question of Roman values as a whole. What *were* some of these "old Roman virtues" that Cicero is alluding to here? Who embodied these virtues? Is Cicero merely indulging in nostalgia for the "good old days" or did something really happen in the late Republic that fundamentally altered what Romans regarded as important? And, despite his defense of Caelius, which side of the debate does *Cicero* seem to be on? As preparation for this discussion, the students might be asked to read (either in Latin or in English) one of Seneca's moral epistles or selections from the early books of Livy in which a similar concern is raised about the loss of those values that made Rome great.[7]

The sociological study of the *Pro Caelio* also permits the teacher to compare Cicero's speech to Catullus' poetry. Catullus, Caelius, and Clodia were all contemporaries, all members of the same social class, all highly educated, and all representatives of the same general values. When Cicero condemns Clodia for her love affairs, students will naturally be reminded of Catullus' poems to "Lesbia" and the love affairs that are reflected in them. But it is also possible to read the *Pro Caelio* in conjunction with Catullus 4 (in praise of Catullus' yacht), 9 (the poet's friend Veranius is warmly welcomed back upon his return from Spain), 10 (Catullus is caught in a lie about bringing litter-bearers back from Bithynia), 12 (Asinius Marrucinus is humorously accused of stealing napkins at a party), 13 (Fabullus is invited to a dinner at Catullus' house . . . if he brings the food), 44 (in praise of Catullus' Sabine farm), 45 (the love of Septimius and Acme), 49 (Catullus' humorous acknowledgment of his gratitude to Cicero), 53 (a lampoon of the lofty oratorical style used in law courts), and 84 (a satire of Arrius' mispronunciations). What do poems like this indicate about Catullus and his circle? How did members of this group spend their time? What sorts of activities did they regard as important? How might Cicero (or even Ap. Claudius Caecus) have felt about Catullus' brand of poetry?

In this way, by comparing the subjects discussed in the poetry of Catullus to those discussed in the *Pro Caelio*, students will come to understand the values of rich, young Romans like Caelius, Catullus, and Clodia. Furthermore, the moral indignation that Cicero demonstrates when referring to Clodia provides insight into how the young aristocracy would have been regarded by many in Rome who were not comfortable with the "new morality."

The students may even discover that there are parallels to this situation today. How are the values reflected in current popular music different from those appearing in certain segments of the press? If a lawyer had to plead a case before a judge and jury, which set of values would the lawyer wish to reflect? The sociological study of the *Pro Caelio* thus permits the teacher to relate this speech, not only to the poetry of Catullus, but also to current situations with which the students are likely to be familiar.[8]

The Rhetorical Study

A third approach that may be taken towards the *Pro Caelio* is to examine how Cicero seeks to prove Caelius' innocence. What points does Cicero regard as relevant to his case? What sort of arguments does he make when his evidence is weak? Which of the charges against Caelius does Cicero prefer to ignore? Since Caelius was acquitted, it is clear that the Romans who heard Cicero found his case to be compelling. But was it the sort of presentation that would be admitted into a court of law today?

At the end of section 22 and the beginning of section 23, Cicero indicates how he intends to demonstrate the innocence of his client:

Equidem vos abducam a testibus neque huius iudici veritatem quae mutari nullo modo potest in voluntate testium conlocari sinam quae facillime fingi, nullo negotio flecti ac detorqueri potest. Argumentis agemus, signis luce omni clarioribus crimina refellemus; res cum re, causa cum causa, ratio cum ratione pugnabit. Itaque illam partem causae facile patior graviter et ornate a M. Crasso peroratam de seditionibus Neapolitanis, de Alexandrinorum pulsatione Puteolana, de bonis Pallae.

For my part, I intend to spare you from the testimony of witnesses. The truth of the case is inalterable and I won't allow it to be manipulated by witnesses. You know how their testimony can be coerced, twisted, and distorted. I prefer to use logic. I'll refute the charges with proofs clearer than light itself. I'll match fact with fact, argument with argument, reason with reason. I'm pleased that the part of this case dealing with the riots at Naples, the attacks upon the Alexandrians at Pozzuoli, and the property of Pallas has been handled so completely and eloquently by my colleague, M. Crassus. [He has done so well that I won't bother rehashing all of that.]

From these statements, it is possible to conclude the following:

1. **That Cicero did not intend to call any witnesses during his speech.** In fact, however, Cicero did rely up the evidence of one, and possibly two, witnesses. Some manuscripts indicate that, even before Cicero made the statement above, one witness had already been called (section 19).[9] Moreover, no one doubts that the testimony of L. Lucceius was later read to the court (section 55). The students might be asked, therefore, how they would react to a lawyer who announced in his opening argument that he would call no witnesses in defense of his client. How, the teacher might continue, would they react if he then proceeded to do so anyway?

2. **That Cicero intended to use reason to refute the charges that had been brought against Caelius.** This is a line of reasoning that Greek rhetoricians called the argument *kata ta eikota* ("according to probability") and Cicero uses it extensively in the *Pro Caelio*. For instance, sections 56-66 consist of a large number of questions designed to make the prosecution's case seem improbable. Why would Caelius have relied upon *slaves* to carry out the poisoning since this assignment was so important? What was the point of having the poison handed over in public at the Senian Baths rather than at a private house? Is it not ridiculous to think that the supposed witnesses could have remained hidden in a public bath? How could P. Licinius, whom the prosecution claimed to have handed over the poison, have escaped from this large number of witnesses? Cicero never disproves the occurrence of any of these things. His goal is merely to make them seem ridiculous and thus unlikely.

3. **That Cicero intended to refute each allegation that had been made by the prosecution.** Cicero does, in fact, provide a systematic refutation of each of the minor charges introduced by Caelius' accusers. Thus he spends a great deal of time countering the claims that Caelius had become alienated from his father, that Caelius was disliked by his fellow townsmen, that Caelius was singularly immoral, that Caelius was a close friend of Catiline, and that Caelius was

deeply in debt. But he never does anything like this for the charge that Caelius was somehow involved in the assassination of Dio. And that is the central issue of the case! By dealing with lesser matters in some detail and then by *claiming* that the entire charge has been refuted, Cicero leaves the impression that he has undermined every claim of his opponents.

4. **That Cicero intended to ignore those aspects of the case that had already been handled by Crassus.** This, unfortunately, is one promise that Cicero *keeps*. As a result, almost nothing is known about the role that the "property of Pallas" played in this case or about the riots at Naples and Caelius' part in the assault upon the Alexandrians.

What Cicero does *not* reveal in this summary of his strategy is the basic rhetorical approach that he will adopt to clear Caelius of the charges. This rhetorical approach may be summarized as follows:

- *"If Caelius is such a terrible person, why were charges never filed against him before this?"* Cicero explicitly asks this question in section 19. Even when it remains unexpressed, however, this is one of the central doubts that Cicero wishes to leave in the minds of the jury.

- *"Clodia is really responsible for the accusations against Caelius and she is so immoral that she ought not to be believed."* Because of his personal connections to Herennius and the family of Atratinus, Cicero went out of his way to avoid attacking the prosecutors personally. (See especially sections 1-2, 7-8, and 25-30.) On the other hand, Cicero establishes Clodia as a "red herring": he first argues that the charges against Caelius really were her idea and then proceeds to assassinate her character.

- *"Boys will be boys."* Cicero's attacks upon the morality of Clodia create a logical problem for him. If she is so wanton, why did Caelius become involved with her? Why this does not mean that Caelius himself is as immoral as she is? To get himself out of this dilemma, Cicero is compelled to adopt a "double standard." He argues that the same activities that were merely youthful high spirits for Caelius were evidence of deep spiritual corruption for Clodia. Moreover, Caelius' libertinism was all in the past (perhaps a few months ago?) while Clodia's immorality continues into the present.

As the students consider these arguments, they might be asked to cite specific examples of Cicero using such rhetorical devices in the *Pro Caelio*. Does the orator's reliance upon such "tricks" suggest that his case was weak? Or is he merely "playing to the audience"? (On the latter point, see Geffcken.) What other rhetorical devices can the students discover in Cicero's arguments? How many of them would be permissible in a court of law today? How many of them appear to be introduced merely in an effort to distract the jury?

By approaching the *Pro Caelio* in this way, therefore, students are encouraged to analyze the logic of Cicero's argumentation. In so doing, they will learn to improve their own techniques of persuasion and to master devices that they may use elsewhere . . . including, perhaps, in the essays they will write for the Advanced Placement examination!

* * * * *

No matter which of these three approaches a teacher chooses to adopt, there are certain procedures that should always be followed in the AP course:

1. Assignments, quizzes, and examinations should be modeled as closely as possible upon the format of the Advanced Placement examination itself. This format is outlined in the College Board's course description booklet (College Board, 20, 22, 24, and 26). Constructing exercises in this way helps both to acquaint students with the sorts of question that they will encounter on the actual examination and to reduce their anxiety about the test by acquainting them with its format well in advance.

2. Each day's work should include at least a small amount of "sight translation" either in the *Pro Caelio* itself or in some related text. Few students will find it possible to memorize all of the passages of Cicero and Catullus that are required for the examination. As a result, practice in translation and analysis of unseen passages improves the skills that they are likely to need when taking the actual exam. Recommended passages to be translated at sight include sections 51-78 of the *Pro Caelio*, selections from other works by Cicero, excerpts from Livy or Seneca, and poems by Catullus not required by the AP syllabus. (For specific recommendations on passages to be translated at sight, see Buller, pp. 17 and 21, note 3.)

3. At least once during the course, students should be required to deliver part of this speech orally, both in Latin and in translation. Oral delivery of the text helps students to develop a sense of Cicero's rhythms and to appreciate the *Pro Caelio* as a work of oratory. Moreover, it provides an important exercise in declamation that they may not be receiving in their other courses.

Prepared in this way, the Advanced Placement course in Latin Literature becomes a valuable experience even for those students who decide not to take the AP exam. It improves their facility at translating difficult Latin, demonstrates a specific approach towards understanding a major work ofclassical literature, and provides opportunities for the parallel study of such apparently diverse authors as Catullus and Cicero.

Notes

1. Much of this information is provided by the *Pro Caelio* itself where Cicero summarizes its various provisions at the beginning of the speech.

2. Dio's goal was to persuade the Senate not to restore the Egyptian king, Ptolemy Auletes, to the throne after he had been driven from power by his own people in 58 B.C.

3. This Clodius is *not* to be confused with Clodia's brother, P. Clodius Pulcher. He was probably the latter's freedman.

4. This is the booklet that is widely known as the "acorn book," so called from the gray logo of an acorn and oak leaf that appears on its front cover.

5. Englert's commentary on the *Pro Caelio* is available for $6.00 (not including postage) from the Bryn Mawr Commentaries, Thomas Library, Bryn Mawr College, Bryn Mawr, PA, 19010. The Thomas Library does not require payment in advance; invoices are included with the shipment. Orders may also be sent by fax (215-526-7475) and are usually filled within a week.

6. The required poems are 1, 2, 2b, 3, 4, 5, 7, 8, 9, 10, 11, 12, 13, 22, 37, 31, 34, 35, 36, 43, 44, 45, 46, 49, 50, 51, 53, 62, 70, 72, 73, 75, 76, 83, 84, 85, 86, 87, 92, 95, 95b, 96, 101, 107, 109. Some versions of the syllabus do include poem 77 and, because of its reference to Caelius, it should be read in any case.

7. In particular, it may be useful for students to read sections 9-10 of Livy's preface where the historian talks about the same sort of moral decay that Cicero is discussing in the *Pro Caelio*, Book 2.12-13 in which the heroism of Mucius Scaevola saves Rome, and Book 29.6-9 in which the accomplishments (and faults!) of Ap. Claudius Caecus are discussed.

8. There are also other Roman values that teachers may wish to explore in a sociological study of the *Pro Caelio*. For instance, students may be asked to consider what this speech reveals about the value given to education by upper class Romans. (See especially sections 9, 11, and 45-47.) What was the attitude of the Romans towards the Greeks? (See especially section 40.) What was their attitude towards women and slaves? (See especially sections 57 and 68.)

9. Some editors believe, however, that the notation DE TESTE FUFIO is not genuine. See, for instance, Englert *Pro Caelio* 41 note 19.20.

References

Austin, R. G. *Pro M. Caelio Oratio*, third edition. Oxford: Clarendon Press, 1960.

Buller, Jeffrey L. "*O Tempora! O Mores!* Teaching Cicero in High Schools Today," 1-23 in Robert M. Terry, ed., *Dimension: Language '92-'93: Foreign Languages: Internationalizing the Future*. Valdosta, GA: Southern Conference on Language Teaching, 1993.

The College Board. *Advanced Placement Course Description: Latin*. Princeton: College Entrance Examination Board, 1993.

Englert, Walter. *Bryn Mawr Commentary on the* **Pro Caelio**. Bryn Mawr, PA: Bryn Mawr Commentaries, 1990.

Geffcken, Katherine. *Comedy in the* **Pro Caelio**. Mnemosyne supplement 30. Leiden, 1973.

Glare, P.G.W., ed. *Oxford Latin Dictionary*. Oxford: Clarendon Press, 1982.

Skinner, Marilyn B. "Clodia Metelli," *Transactions of the American Philological Association*, 113 (1983): 273-287.

The Basic Components of FLES*:
Communication and Culture

Gladys C. Lipton
University of Maryland – Baltimore County Campus

Abstract

The major thrusts of all types of FLES* programs (Sequential FLES, FLEX and Immersion) are communication and culture. The communication section deals with the person-to-person interactions which reflect the child's world. The culture section explores the ways in which children can gain insights into cultural concepts in a world different from their own. This article examines these two key components, giving specific examples of how they are implemented in the FLES* classroom.

Introduction

FLES* programs today are the result of phenomenal growth in the 1980's and the 1990's. Many parents, administrators, and school board members are enthusiastic about all types of FLES* programs for a number of reasons, based on research studies, which will be cited below. Some decision makers are beginning to understand that the second language acquisition process requires many years of study. They are beginning to recognize the need for starting foreign language study in the elementary school, if we are aiming at the development of a large cadre of students with foreign language proficiency skills at the high school and college levels.

Types of FLES* Programs

There are three types of program models: Sequential FLES, FLEX or Exploratory, and Immersion. Each program model has different goals and expected outcomes, and each program model attempts to achieve the goals through a variety of approaches. However, all three program models are concerned with the two basic elements of FLES*: communication and culture.

Before proceeding, it is important to clarify the terms which are used throughout this paper and which appear on the FLES* brochure which was developed, funded and is distributed by the American Association of Teachers of French and the American Association of Teachers of Spanish and Portuguese[1]:

> **FLES*** is the overall 'umbrella' for all types of elementary school foreign language programs in grades K-8.
>
> **Sequential FLES** is an introduction to one foreign language for two or more years, with a systematic development of language skills (listening, speaking, reading, writing, and culture) within the parameters of themes, topics, or content areas. Good theme-related fluency is expected (if scheduled five times a week, thirty minutes or more a day) for four or more years.
>
> **FLEX** is an introduction to one or more foreign languages, with few language skills expected. Limited fluency is expected with a once or twice a week program which emphasizes limited language acquisition and extensive cultural awareness.
>
> **Immersion** is the use of the foreign language throughout the school day by teachers and students, for teaching the various subjects of the elementary school curriculum. Good fluency in the foreign language is expected after four or more years in the program.

Other countries are interested in beginning foreign language study in the primary grades. Canada, because of its specific socio-economic-political needs, has had a strong interest in starting foreign language programs earlier, although their rationale has had a different focus from that of programs in the United States. Mexico is experimenting with foreign language in first grade, and many European countries, such as France, England, Norway, and others, are piloting programs of foreign languages in the primary grades.

Why FLES*?

There are a number of research studies which support the various reasons for FLES*. Space does not permit an extensive review of the literature on this topic, but the following points, documented by research, present the case for FLES*:

1. Children have the ability to learn and excel in the pronunciation of a foreign language. Several authors have documented this point (Dulay, Burt, Krashen).

2. FLES* has a favorable effect on foreign language study later in high school and college. A longitudinal study on this point was conducted by Carroll.

3. Children who have studied a foreign language in elementary school achieve expected gains in reading, language arts, and mathematics. The best source for documentation on this point is Rafferty.

4. Children who have studied a foreign language show greater cognitive development in such areas as mental flexibility, creativity, and divergent thinking. Research on these topics was conducted by Landry.

5. Children who have studied a foreign language develop a sense of cultural pluralism to people from other cultures. Useful studies on this topic were conducted in Canada by Lambert and Tucker.

6. Children studying a foreign language have an improved self-concept and sense of achievement in school. Genesee researched this topic in Canada.

For a more extensive review of the research, readers are directed to a book which helps administrators understand the research base for FLES* (Lipton, 34-42). Regarding FLES* research, we have a number of well-designed research studies from the 1960s, some of which have been replicated in the 1980s. An extremely comprehensive study in Louisiana by Rafferty resulted in positive documentation for FLES* programs. We are in urgent need for others to conduct research studies. Studies which are not carefully designed and which do not control *all* of the variables are particularly harmful to FLES* programs as well as to other levels of foreign language programs.

We also need research on the many intangible benefits to children through participation in a FLES* program. These are not usually measurable, but they indicate valuable skills, abilities, and perceptions which students develop as a result of participating in a FLES* program. FLES* teachers report that children's listening skills are greatly improved, their relationships with their foreign-language-speaking peers are enhanced, their goegraphical and historical concepts are broadened, and their attitude toward school, in general, is more positive.

FLES* teachers are generally not trained to conduct research, and perhaps that should be part of the teacher preparation process. FLES* teachers, however, working with research professionals, can participate in all types of FLES* research, so that the field can benefit from additional documentation and objective evaluation.

It is interesting to note on the topic of research on FLES* that there is an on-going spirited discussion of immersion in Canada by several authors (Hammerly and Rehorick, Edwards). Rehorick and Edwards have compiled a well-documented book on the controversy of whether or not immersion, as it exists today in Canada, is effective. The opinions of both sides of the controversy are presented in this little-known document.

Communication, the First Basic Component of FLES*

Person-to-person communication (both oral and written, depending on the goals of the program model) has long been a major goal of elementary school foreign language programs as evidenced by the thematic units which appear regularly in FLES* curricula across the decades. Such topics as greetings, family, friends, games and leisure time activities, food, health, sports, travel, etc., have formed the basis for all kinds of conversations, dialogues, total physical response (TPR), and other kinds of classroom activities. This occurs primarily in Sequential FLES and FLEX programs. In immersion programs, the foreign language is the language of communication, as students learn the content of the elementary school curriculum while using the foreign language.

With the advent of new technologies such as international electronic communication, satellite reception and distance learning, CD ROM and virtual reality, person-to-person communication continues to be extremely vital to all types of FLES* programs. The technology will be a major factor in furthering person-to-person international communication, provided that there are funds for supporting this technology in elementary schools.

Although FLES* programs utilize some interdisciplinary aspects and some reinforcement of activities of the regular elementary school curriculum content (content-based instruction), the major focus on real-life communication is dominant. As an example of interdisciplinary activities, some classrooms will, at some point, discuss the needs and life cycle of toads, as an example. But one wonders how many students are interested in discussing toads as the focus of their conversations? On the other hand, children are interested in the many topics in other classes and throughout the school. Such interdisciplinary activities as reinforcing the celebration of Columbus Day, for example, may be a useful integration of Social Studies and the foreign language. Plans for a school-wide spring festival may provide additional communicative activities for the FLES* classroom. FLES* teachers are encouraged to reach into many different aspects of the elementary school curriculum.

Many surveys have been made about the interests of elementary school age children. Not surprisingly, they are interested in their families and their home, their day-to-day activities, school, teachers, and other students, TV programs and movies, cartoons, and comics. They are also captivated by video game heroes such as the Mario Brothers, Sonic, Sewer Shark, sports personalities, and all the real-life activities encompassing the world of children. The strength of all kinds of FLES* programs is in the potential for capturing in the FLES* classroom, the "native-language kid-talk" (N.L.K.T.) which normally takes place in and outside the elementary school. Not a new concept, but a new term developed by the author, this approach of focussing upon the lives and interactions of children has been helpful in providing a solid base for FLES* programs.

The most successful FLES* programs are those which capitalize on children's N.L.K.T. and their interests, and make these topics the nucleus of the program. How is this done? This is accomplished with theme-related units using such techniques as cooperative learning groups, paired activities, learner-centered activities, individualization of instruction using some kind of technology,games with a heavy emphasis on real-life situations (such as market scenes or restaurant scenarios, etc.) Many FLES* teachers use cooperative learning groups for the development of conversations, skits, and other real-life person-to-person communication situations. Others use paired activities where students are able to help one another through partner practice.

By using N.L.K.T. as the basis for strengthening person-to-person communication, teachers discover quickly that children do not regularly communicate in complete sentences. That means that some rejoinders may be one word answers. There will be many other occasions when students will be using complete sentences. Children need to learn the difference between casual and formal talk.

The use of a Situation Box is an excellent way to stimulate the flow of language particulary with pairs or small groups. Some examples of situations might include:

1. What do you do when you spill your soda at the movies?

2. What happens when you get lost at the mall?

3. What happens when you are at a party and you get sick?

4. What do you do when you forget your friend's birthday?

5. What do you say when you receive a gift which you do not like?

Successful FLES* teachers make it a point to include in each lesson many opportunities for all students to use the foreign language. This is particularly difficult to do when class time is short and students have not had much exposure to the foreign language. Planning for even three to four minutes during each lesson for students to work in pairs and/or groups will affirm for students that they are making progress in their ability to communicate in the foreign language.

An important aspect of teaching communication is that of assessing student progress. The most effective way is to keep a variety of records of student performance in a portfolio of some kind. Cassette recordings, creative pictures, tests, short dictations, class videotapes, creative poetry or short play, TPR commands, inventive advertisements, jokes, and short stories, all in the foreign language, are examples of the kinds of student work that might become part of an individual portfolio. Class portfolios are also helpful in providing evidence of the effectiveness of the communicative skills of the class.

But, it must be remembered that so much of what happens in FLES* classrooms does not fit neatly into a portfolio. Students engage in market scenes, they write to pen pals via electronic transmission, they are involved in dramatic presentations, they go on field trips and gather all kinds of information, they work in cooperative learning groups to plan and execute a class celebration of "Oktoberfest," for example, and many other examples of activities which enrich and enliven the FLES* program.

Students perform plays and musicals in school and also at outside group meetings, such as Kiwanis clubs and other business and social groups. They participate in national contests, such as the AATF FLES* *Grand Concours*, and the AATF and AATSP national FLES* poster contests, and other competitions such as statewide FLES* spelling bees. They celebrate National FLES* Day, which is the first Monday of National Foreign Language Week, to denote that FLES* is the beginning of the foreign language sequence.

Do FLES* teachers ever give paper-and-pencil tests? Of course they do! The documentation of student progress, however, needs to be much broader, so that there is a clear indication of students' communicative progress from year to year and from school to school. Readers interested in specific information about using a variety of class tests for the purpose of developing accuracy are referred to an article on FLES* assessment by Valette.

It is clear that while children enjoy using thematic topics of N.L.K.T., they still have to learn how to speak to adults in real-life situations. No matter which approaches are used, if the goal is person-to-person communication on topics of interest to children, the program is certain to be headed in the right direction.

Culture

A second imperative for all types of FLES* programs is the goal of teaching culture. The teaching of culture in FLES* programs is what may be termed as people-to-people culture, rather than culture devoted solely to the teaching of names of cities, rivers and mountains, etc. Can anyone teach culture at the elementary school level? Can children be able to grasp such sophisticated topics as cross-cultural concepts and understandings? Unfortunately, it is easier to teach facts about culture than it is to teach cultural sensitivity and cross-cultural understanding.

Here, again, the focus is on relating the cultural content to the students' interests in day-to-day activities. Elementary school students are keenly interested in and curious about their peers in other countries: How do they dress? What do they eat? What do they do in school? What kind of television programs do they watch? The teaching of culture can be accomplished by making comparisons between the target culture and our own. Happily, all three types of FLES* program models afford numerous opportunities to include cultural concepts and activities in the program.

It has often been said that language is culture and culture is language. This simply means that linguistic components and cultural elements cannot be separated. It also means that the practice of devoting one lesson a month to the acqusition of cultural facts about culture(s) is not the recommended approach. What is recommended is the infusion of cultural components in each lesson. It is a hands-on approach involving role-playing, examining artifacts, examining ways in which students may explore and try to find out, interviewing people, and then comparing ideas so that no student in the class develops a stereotypical view of the target culture or cultures. Using an example of looking at Hispanic culture, students need to understand a major concept that not all people who speak the same foreign language (even though they may speak it similarly) have the same cultural characteristics. People in Madrid, for example, may have different daily routines from those in Mexico City.

In teaching about a target culture or cultures, teachers at the FLES* level need to be sure to avoid the use of the words "all" and "always." They need to encourage children to check several sources, and to evaluate different source materials. Here is where the use of authentic materials proves to be invaluable, even if the language level is above that of the FLES* students. So much information can be gleaned from looking at and comparing different pictures in newspapers and magazines.

Cooperative learning teams, working on different assignments about the culture, can first learn how to make hypotheses about the foreign culture(s) and then gather all kinds of information about such daily activities in the target culture(s) as daily routines, family life, food, family, school, and leisure-time activities, different professions, customs and ceremonies, and many other topics.

What are some specific techniques of teaching culture at the FLES* level? These include such procedures (to mention just a few examples) as having groups of children

- consult materials in a cross-cultural center with books, magazines, music, videos, task sheets, learning modules, etc.

- participate in the making of a cross-cultural mural or collage.

- participate in developing plans for a pretend class trip to a country in the foreign culture. After the "pretend" trip, a "real" trip to the foreign language-speaking country may be planned.

- work on a year-long activity involving, for example, a German language cultural calendar for children, which might include birth dates of famous people, holiday celebrations, historical events, current happenings, etc.

- explore the range of proverbs and sayings in a foreign culture. Here is an excellent example of how language and culture intertwine, particularly where there are proverbs which indicate one position, and other proverbs which indicate the direct opposite, just as we have in English. For example, we say "The early bird catches the worm," but we also say "Better late than never."

- plan a "Culture freeze" where, after doing some research about an important event, students re-enact a selected historical event. At one point the action is stopped, and that is why it is called a "Culture freeze." The favorite event selected by most students of French, for example, seems to be the guillotining of Marie Antoinette!

- "invent a culture," creating such characteristics as a description of its land, the people, celebrations, customs, government, food, water, language, etc.

It is important for children to learn that there often is not a word-for-word translation of thoughts in English, nor is there an exact foreign language translation for each word of English. Furthermore, they need to learn that words which have foreign language equivalents do not always convey the same concept. Consider the situation where students are seeking a translation of the word for "bread." They will learn, if they consult a dictionary, that the French equivalent is *le pain*. The FLES* teacher must help students understand that *le pain* does not really mean a cellophane-wrapped package of sliced bread, but that it is probably a long French loaf. This is a good example of the concept of the language-culture connection in the FLES* classroom.

Conclusion

Needless to say, the two basic elements of a FLES* program (communication and culture) are not the only important aspects of successful FLES* programs. Without effective, trained teachers, without specific goals for the program which are in keeping with the school and school district goals, without access to the program available to *all* interested students, without challenging materials, without strong parental support, without strong administrative support, without a well-planned scope and sequence with plans for articulation at the next school level, without meaningful documentation of the success of the program, without coordination of the program, the program is not viable. Readers interested in a discussion of the characteristics of successful FLES* programs are directed to ACTFL's "Characteristics of effective elementary school FL programs."

Note

1. *Why FLES*?* Brochure, distributed by AATF, 57 E. Armory Ave., Champaign, IL 61820 and AATSP, University of Northern Colorado, Greeley, CO 80639.

References

Bernhardt, E., ed. *Life in Language Immersion Classrooms*. Clevedon (G.B.): Multilingual Matters, Ltd., 1992.

Carroll, J. "Foreign Language Proficiency Levels Attained by Language Majors near Graduation from College." *Foreign Language Annals* 1 (1967): 131-35.

"Characterisitcs of effective elementary school FL programs." *ACTFL Newsletter*, Spring (1992): 6,9.

Cribari, S. "FLES*—It's Elementary, My Dear Watson!" *Collaborare*, Vol. viii, No. 3 (1993): 1-3.

Curtain, H. and C. Pesola. *Languages and Children: Making the Match*. Reading, MA: Addison-Wesley, 1994.

Dulay, H., Burt, M. and S. Krashen. *Language Two*. New York: Oxford University Press, 1982.

Genesee, F. *Learning Through Two Languages*. Rowley, MA: Newbury House, 1987.

Hammerly, H. *French Immersion: Myths and Reality*. Calgary, Alberta: Detselig Enterprises Ltd., 1989.

Kennedy, D. and W. DeLorenzo. *Complete Guide to Exploratory Foreign Language Programs*. Lincolnwood, IL: National Textbook Co., 1985.

Landry, R. "A Comparison of Second Language Learners and Monolinguals on Divergent Thinking Tasks at the Elementary School Level." *Modern Language Journal* 58 (1974): 10-15.

Lipton, G. "Enseigner la culture dans la classe de langue étrangère au niveau élémentaire," 175-179 in Robert C. Lafayette, ed. *Culture et Enseignement du Français*. Paris: Didier, 1994.

_____. *The Administrator's Guide to FLES* Programs*. Lincolnwood, IL: National Textbook Co., 1992.

_____. *Practical Handbook to Elementary Foreign Language Programs, including FLES, FLEX and Immersion*. Lincolnwood, IL: National Textbook Co., 1988, 1992.

_____, ed. *Evaluating FLES* Programs*. Report of the National FLES* Commission of AATF. Champaign, IL: AATF, 1992.

Lundin, J. and D. Dolson, eds. *Studies in Immersion Education*. Sacramento: California State Dept. of Education, 1984.

Rafferty, E. *Second Language Study and Basic Skills in Louisiana*. Baton Rouge: Louisiana Dept. of Education, 1986.

Rehorick, S. and V. Edwards. *French Immersion: Process, Product and Perspectives*. Welland, Ontario: *Canadian Modern Language Review*, 1992.

Riordan, K. "Public Relations: Inside and Outside," 64-67 in G. Lipton, ed. *Innovations in FLES* Programs*. Champaign, IL: AATF, 1990.

Lambert, W. and G. Tucker. *Bilingual Education of Children*. Rowley, MA: Newbury House, 1972.

Valette, R. "Using Class Quizzes to Promote the Linguistic Accuracy of Younger Learners," 1-9 in G. Lipton, ed., *Evaluating FLES* Programs*. Champaign, IL: AATF, 1991.

4

Multiculturalism in Elementary French Textbooks

Flore Zéphir
University of Missouri-Columbia

Curriculum in Transition

Multiculturalism is at the heart of current academic discourse. Berman (1992) and Aufderheide (1992) offer several significant articles that underscore the intensity of the debate about the place of multiculturalism or cultural diversity in the curriculum. Indeed, major universities, including SUNY, Harvard, Stanford, and Duke, are orchestrating important changes in their general education curriculum to reflect cultural pluralism. The present academic trend is also stongly articulated by the foreign language teaching profession. The 1992 Northeast Conference on the Teaching of Foreign Languages emphasizes "languages for a multicultural world in transition" (Byrnes 1992, vii). García (1992, 1) recognizes that "multilingualism and multiculturism are the defining characteristics of society."

Given the pluralistic nature of the world, the need to modify the traditional curriculum so as to include the study of various cultures outside the dominant society or traditional mainstream, becomes imperative. With regard to the teaching of foreign languages, multiculturalism could mean the inclusion in the traditional syllabus of the varieties of the target languages spoken by non-dominant communities, and the inclusion of the cultures of these particular peoples. The attention to non-dominant groups in the teaching of foreign languages is well-echoed by García (1992, 18) when she writes, "And so whether we teach French, German, Italian, or

Spanish, our understanding must be not only of those languages in their dominant contexts, but also of the ethnolinguistic minorities within those countries."

Specifically for the teaching of French, multiculturalism could be achieved through a certain familiarity with the French language of Africa, the Caribbean, Southeast Asia, the Indian and Pacific Ocean islands, and of the cultures of these francophone regions. With respect to the francophone world, it is clear that cultural diversity is becoming one of its salient features. Indeed, an article published in *L'Express* (reproduced in Rosenthal, de Verneil, and DuVerlie (1993, 482) teacher's edition) states that before the end of the century, among the francophones, the French people of the *hexagone* will become a minority. The article goes on to say that the number of francophones in countries in Africa and the Indian Ocean should double by the year 2000, rising from 27 millions to more than 55 millions. These important facts unequivocally suggest that the culture of France should not dominate the French textbooks. The French numerical minority cannot adequately represent the totality of the multicultural francophone world.

In the pages that follow, the critical issue that will be addressed is to what extent current college elementary French textbooks contribute to the promotion of multiculturalism. Whose language, whose culture, that is the question. The answer to this important question can be found in a careful analysis of thirteen current first-year college French textbooks published between 1990 and 1993.[1]

Multiculturalism in First-Year French Textbooks

First, it is important to acknowledge that cultural matters do receive a great deal of coverage in the textbooks examined (*Allons-y, Voilà, Invitation, Découverte et Création, Rendez-vous, Entre-Amis, Objectif France, Ça marche, Situations et Contextes, Deux Mondes, Contacts, Rapports, En Avant*).[2] Moreover, culture and language are well integrated throughout the various chapters, and it is evident that the authors have sought successfully to "represent a panorama of French life" through the functional aspect of language presented in realistic situations.[3] At this time, the relevant question is to discern from the overall amount of cultural coverage how much is devoted to francophone as opposed to "hexagonal" perspectives. A perusal of the tables of contents of the above-cited texts reveals that the majority of topics covered in most of these books tend to focus on hexagonal matters such as French schools and universities, French students, French identity and lifestyle, how to travel in France,

French food and cuisine, France and its climate, family life in France, French television, health and exercise in France, French fashion and elegance, French wines and cheeses, French cities, medicine in France, vacations in France, and transportation in France.

Overall not a great deal of time is spent outside the *hexagone* to appreciate the living language and culture of non-dominant francophone societies. Indeed, topics such as Tunisian schools and universities, family life in Cameroon, Senegalese food and cuisine, health pratices in francophone Africa, or leisure activities in the francophone West Indies do not abound in these textbooks.

The concerns for multicultural coverage expressed in this paper can be grouped into three categories: (1) the tendency to limit the francophone coverage to "facts-only"[4]; (2) the tendency to limit this coverage to one particular skill—reading; and (3) the insufficiency of multicultural activities.

Because of space limitations, a tedious review of every text examined cannot be done.[5] However, illustrative examples are offered to highlight the above-mentioned concerns. For instance, the authors of textbook A allocate about ten pages of their six hundred page text to multicultural (francophone) coverage. At the end of chapter 4, a short *portrait* of a Senegalese, Massyla Fodéba, is offered, followed by a *profil* (list of facts) of *le Sénégal*. Morocco receives some coverage at the end of chapter 8 in the form of a short portrait of M. Ahmed Abdida and a list of facts about this country. The multicultural tour continues in chapter 11 with a similar portrait of the Guadeloupean Marie-Claude Étienne and a list of facts about Guadeloupe, and ends with a set of pictures of *le monde francophone*, which includes *l'Afrique francophone* and *les Antilles*, on pages 480-483. While the multicultural coverage of this well-received text is mostly limited to a set of geographical and historical facts, it is worth noting that the authors attempt to integrate some francophone perspectives with the teaching of linguistic materials. For example, on page 232 (chapter 6), the authors design an interesting activity involving numbers with a few facts on Mali and include a picture. On page 355 (chapter 9), time is practiced through the use of the timetable of the *Union des transports aériens (U.T.A.)* and *Air Afrique* flights between Paris and Niamey (capital of Niger). More activities of this type are needed in order to integrate adequately francophone perspectives with the teaching of elementary French.

The tendency to limit francophone culture to historical and geographical facts is also manifest in textbook E. A short history of *francophonie* is drafted on page 508, and exercises are included in the next page.

Le français en Afrique is the topic of the cultural reading offered on page 527. The same observations about francophone coverage can be made with regard to textbook F. Students are exposed mostly to geographical and historical facts about Senegal through a reading titled *l'histoire du Sénégal*. However, it is worth stating that the authors do mention in their reading selection certain traditional customs (clothing and language), and certain intellectual phenomena (the *négritude* movement of Senghor) about Senegal. The coverage of Morocco and Martinique is done through facts only.

Textbook B presents a fair amount of non-hexagonal point of view mainly through a series of *magazines francophones* inserted throughout the book. The magazines pertinent to our discussion include magazines 1, 2, 4, 5, and 6. On the first page of magazine 1 appears a portrait (list of biographical information) of the Senegalese writer, Birago Diop. Page 2 features a very popular African musical group, and the next page lists some geographical facts about Senegal and Morocco. In magazine 2, one can read statistics about *francophonie,* and look at a map of the *DOM-TOM* (French overseas departments and territories). Magazine 4, which is a dossier on immigration, features various successful immigrants of West Indian, African and northern African origin. On page 3 of magazine 5 is an abstract of a short story by a Cameroonian freelance writer. Magazine 6 offers a profile of a Martinican, a Malian, and a Malgache writer.

While these magazines certainly offer valuable multicultural information, they include no activities. This unfortunate omission might suggest that they are not an essential part of the text and are to be used only when all other material has been covered. The addition of activities will be desirable as they will enable students to reflect on and use meaningfully this information. If we take the dossier on immigration presented in magazine 4, various communicative activities can be devised around the topic. For instance, students could be asked to conduct an interview with a francophone immigrant. (Finding such a person should not be too difficult in a school or university environment). Their task would be to find out when the immigrant came to the U.S., where he/she first went upon arrival in the U.S., why he/she came to the U.S., and how long he/she intends to stay. Such an activity enables students to practice a particular linguistic structure (question formation, in this instance) in an authentic situation that enhances multicultural perspectives. A variation of this activity could be for the instructor to invite a francophone immigrant to come to his/her class as a guest speaker. Students would then ask the speaker questions about his/her immigration experience. Many additional activities, including writing tasks, could be developed to engage students in cross-cultural analysis as well.

In our discussion of multicultural activities, it is relevant to note that the authors of textbook G suggest some very interesting activities. Following each of their multicultural *fenêtres* (windows) that open onto the francophone world, they devise several research activities that can be done in groups. In addition, they offer several oral activities that include discussions, interviews, surveys, debates, and panel discussions. Their activities could be a good source of ideas for authors and instructors concerned about enhancing students' multicultural knowledge. Finally, it is pertinent to acknowledge that the readings chosen for incorporation of multicultural content are by and large authentic. Indeed, they include various newspaper articles, poems by Senghor, Damas, and other African and Caribbean writers (textbooks H and M); northern African tales (textbook L); and aspects of Cajun life (the *fais-dodo* and the *calinda* traditions) through the voice of an authentic *cadjine*, Madame Barbara Hébert (textbook J), to recall a few examples.

However, it may be appropriate to caution against the presentation of multicultural perspectives through the European voice. An example of this sort of presentation can be found in textbook I. The authors offer a letter written by a French adolescent, Caroline, to her godparents, the Bordiers, while she is vacationing in Tunisia. From a multicultural point of view, this letter is not very informative. The only information given about Tunisia is that it is a beautiful but a poor country. The remainder of the letter is devoted to personal matters. The letter could be rewritten, but this time, from the perspective of a Tunisian, not a French, adolescent. The young Tunisian girl could be writing a letter to her godparents in which she makes, for example, some comparisons between French and Tunisian life style. The authors of textbook C also offer a non-indigenous voice in their presentation of Reunion. The young French man, Daniel, talks about his impression of the island. The native voice could be more appropriate to offer a real Reunionese perspective. Later in their text, these authors do present the native voice of a Zairean, Kiwele Shamavu, who talks about his childhood memories and shares valuable information about his native land. The indigenous voice is undoubtedly very instrumental in the fostering of multiculturalism. Authors are strongly encouraged to include more instances of this type of presentation in their textbooks.

Discussion

As stated earlier, our content analysis of selected college French textbooks reveals that the presentation of multicultural phenomena is largely based on written texts (readings); and furthermore, it shows that the information presented pertains to "facts-only" and covers what is commonly referred to as "big C" culture. Allen (1985), Kramsch (1988), and Lafayette (1988), among others, have argued that the view of culture should encompass both the small culture, which is the social aspects of daily life, and the big Culture, which comprises geographical, historical, artistic, literary, and intellectual facts. While reading is an effective strategy to impart factual information (big C), it does not actively represent the target people in the performance of their everyday activities (small c). Limiting multiculturalism to a mere exposure to geographical/historical facts through reading selections can lead to a passive, incomplete, and even inaccurate understanding and knowledge of multi-culture. In fact, Crawford-Lange & Lange (1984), Seelye (1984), and Allen (1985) are among those who caution about the limitations of the "facts-only" approach to the teaching of culture. Multiculturalism is a lived concept that could be integrated with the teaching of productive skills as well.

Furthermore, a comparison between the type of cultural information provided for France and for non-European francophone regions is revealing. French culture is brought to life by real French people. Indeed, they are portrayed as they live: they attend school, work, spend time with their families, eat, shop, exercise, play sports, watch television, go out, go on vacation, etc. An attempt is made to initiate students to the French way of life. Additionally, abundant visual support is added, which includes such authentic materials as photographs, pictures, maps, menus, train tickets and schedules, various ads, newspaper clippings, TV guides, postcards, and the like. However, when it comes to societies outside the *hexagone*, one notices an absence of similar materials. Thus one asks what happens in the daily life of the Senegalese, the Zaireans, the Martinicans, or the Guadeloupeans. The multiple facets of their culture are too often reduced to numbers and statistics. Seelye's (1984, 26) definition of culture as "a broad concept that embraces all aspects of the life of man" is not well echoed through this kind of application. In fact, such a presentation may not be very conducive to tolerance and appreciation of multicultural differences.

Suggestions

The importance of textbooks in the instructional enterprise is well documented and cannot be minimized. Olson (1980, 189) argues that the text "remains the bedrock of syllabus design and lesson planning." Lafayette (1988, 47) notes that the "textbooks still constitute (after the teacher) the most important cog in the educational process." Kramsch (1988, 85) calls it "a catalyst for learning." Therefore, it is not unreasonable to require that textbooks become media of multicultural instruction. Their role as major conveyors of multicultural information could be enhanced considerably. To echo the words of Galloway (1992, 97), the inseparability of language and culture must be recognized, and efforts to promote cross-cultural understanding must begin "by recognition of the role of culture in the use of language for communication."[6] In order words, the inclusion of multiculturalism must be done through active (as opposed to passive or receptive) language.

Since active language necessarily entails the interaction of real people, textbooks could begin by including many more interactions or conversations involving participants from non-European francophone regions. For example, in any chapter on French universities, it might be appropriate to have an exchange between two Algerian students studying in France where they engage in a comparison between the French university system and that of Algeria. In the chapter on food, a conversation at an ethnic restaurant or at an ethnic grocery store could be muticulturally informative. Instead of ordering just a *bière* (beer), Kabibi could be ordering a *timbo* or a *simba* (local Zairean beers) and some *foufou* (manioc dish) or *mokasa* (stew made with meat or fish, palm oil, and peanut butter).[7] At the local Tunisian grocery store, Ali could be buying some *semoule* (wheat product) to make his *couscous*. In addition, this chapter could be greatly enhanced by the addition of a few ethnic recipes. In the chapter on recreation, two West Indian friends, Jacqueline and Marjorie, could be deciding between going to see the movie *Rue Case-nègre* or going to listen to the well-known Martinican musical group *Kasav*. In Port-au-Prince, Haiti, Tite-Soeur and Phito, would not take the *métro* but the *tap-tap* (local van).[8]

Second, in addition to conversations, it is strongly suggested that multiculturalism be introduced actively with vocabulary. Instead of presenting solely traditional French food items (well placed in their cultural context), francophone multi-ethnic food could be added to the active repertoire. This could be done, for example, by including in the food section pictures of an open market scene, say in Mali, depicting various vendors with their products. Items like *lambi* (conch), *hareng saur* (type of herring), *avocat* (avocado), *patate* (sweet potato), *foufou, couscous, mangue* (mango), *goyave* (guava), *papaye* (papaya) constitute a few examples of what could be added. The same could be said of vocabulary relating to clothing. Some examples of ethnic items of clothing include *diellaba* (caftan), *hedjab* (long Senegalese dress), *tchador* (scarf), *boubou* (long tunic), and *abacos* (Zairean man's suit). Pictures of all these items could be added to those of the French *complet, tailleur, robe,* and *jupe*.

One notes that several textbooks do mention some of this relevant multicultural information. But for the most part, it tends to be buried in a cultural note at the end of the active material and appears to be intended for passive recognition. Textbook B lists the vocabulary introduced in two sections at the end of each chapter: *vocabulaire de base* (basic vocabulary) and *vocabulaire supplémentaire* (additional vocabulary). In this additional vocabulary section under the rubric *on entend parfois* (one sometimes hears), the authors include other francophone terms and idiomatic expressions. If the teaching of multicultural content is a desirable goal for elementary French textbooks, it is therefore recommended that this information be moved to a more visible location in the text where it could be integrated with the core content.

Third, multiculturalism should be integrated more with the teaching of grammar. As it was done in textbook M (chapter 14), the geographical countries chosen to teach prepositions should reflect the diversity of the multicultural francophone world. Ethnic foods, like those mentioned above, could serve to reinforce the use of the partitive. More activities of the type seen in textbook C (chapter 6, page 232) could be devised to teach numbers, since they involved multicultural factual information. Currency from other francophone regions could also be used to practice these numbers. The agreement of adjectives could be done through activities involving the description of well-known people from multi-cultures, such as Senegal President Senghor or the Martinican musician Harlem Désir.

Fourth, more activities that have a multicultural focus need to be developed and included in textbooks. For example, various composition topics, as well as other writing or speaking tasks, could be organized around a multicultural theme. If we take the multicultural information presented in textbook A through its francophone portraits, it is possible to devise two related communicative activities. The first activity would consist of students interviewing a francophone immigrant, the second one would involve students writing a portrait (similar to those read in the textbook) of the person interviewed.

Finally, it may also be appropriate to encourage instructors to take full advantage of and exploit extensively the multicultural information contained in the textbooks. To suggest one example, pictures can be used actively for the francophone perspectives they offer and serve as a point of departure for various multicultural activities. Indeed, one can find photographs of African and Caribbean open market scenes, of traditional African clothes, and of important and well-known francophone figures. These can certainly be used to teach several social aspects of the daily life of these particular francophone societies. The possibilities for multicultural expansion are endless; and as foreign language teachers, we are urged to explore them seriously in our classrooms. We need to remember that our goal is to teach multi-culture, not to teach about multi-culture.

Conclusion

Kulick and Mather (1993, 900) indicate that the cultural contributions of francophone peoples from around the world is being recognized as a fundamental and integral part of any French language or literature program. While efforts are certainly undertaken to build "francophone cultural literacy,"[9] they are oriented toward the upper division of the curriculum. Kulick and Mather (1993) attempt successfully to remedy this state of affairs and outline a meritorious initiative to integrate francophone studies in the second-year foreign language curriculum. However, foreign language teachers may question the need to wait until the second or third year to introduce multicultural perspectives. In fact, these same researchers admit that "early exposure to any number of the multiple facets of the francophone world can provide language students with important notions that will allow them to comprehend many of the images, colors, and figures of speech that characterize francophone literature" (905). This early exposure should occur in the first semester.

This paper has outlined some of the reasons why first-year French textbooks should strive for early multicultural exposure and has proposed ways to accomplish this. Like Lafayette (1988, 47), this author contends that "the textbook itself represents the most powerful agent for change in language teaching." Additionally, the textbook often represents one of the most valuable sources of information for the teacher, and the student. A textbook that presents a well-balanced selection of francophone societies is a good way to allow multi-culture to actually "visit" the classroom. With the help of French language materials, foreign language programs can become the leaders in a long-overdue change in the direction of multiculturalism.

Notes

1. The textbooks are listed alphabetically by author.

2. Several of these textbooks have appeared in earlier editions. For the purpose of this article, only the most recent edition was examined.

3. These words are borrowed from Jarvis, Bonin, and Birckbichler's (1993) preface to *Invitation*, p.ix.

4. The term "facts-only approach" is borrowed from Lafayette (1988, 54).

5. In the remainder of the paper, textbooks and authors are mentioned by coded letter. A key is provided in the Appendix.

6. Galloway's comments apply very well to our discussion of multiculturalism, and the world "culture" could be easily re-interpreted as "multi-culture."

7. I am indebted to Dr. Tschiswaka Kayembe, a native of Zaïre, for his contribution to the ethnic lexicon.

8. A picture of these *tap-tap* can be found in *Découverte et Création* by Jian and Hester (1990, chapter 22).

9. The expression is borrowed from Kulick and Mather (1993, 900).

References

Allen, Wendy. W. "Toward Cultural Proficiency," 137-66 in Alice C. Omaggio, ed., *Proficiency, Curriculum, Articulation: The Ties that Bind,* Northeast Conference. Middlebury, VT: Northeast Conference Reports, 1985.

Aufderheide, Patricia. *Beyond P.C.: Toward a Politics of Understanding.* St.Paul, MN: Graywolf Press, 1992.

Berman, Paul. *Debating P.C.: The Controversy over Political Correctness on College Campuses.* New York: Dell, 1992.

Bragger, Jeannette D. and Donald B. Rice. *Allons-y: Le français par étapes.* Boston: Heinle & Heinle, 1992.

Byrnes, Heidi. *Languages for a Multicultural World in Transition.* Northeast Conference Reports. Lincolnwood, IL: National Textbook, 1992.

Crawford-Lange, Linda M. and Dale L. Lange. "Doing the Unthinkable in Second-Language Classroom: A Process for the Integration of Language and Culture," 139-77 in Theodore. V. Higgs, ed., *Teaching for Proficiency: The Organizing Principle.* The ACTFL Foreign Language Education Series. Lincolnwood, IL: National Textbook, 1984.

Galloway, Vicki. "Toward a Cultural Reading of Authentic Texts," 87-121 in Heidi Byrnes, ed., *Languages for a Multicultural World in Transition*. Northeast Conference Reports. Lincolnwood, IL: National Textbook, 1992.

García, Ofelia. "Societal Multilingualism in a Multicultural World in Transition," 1-27 in Heidi Byrnes, ed., *Languages for a Multicultural World in Transition*. Northeast Conference Reports. Lincolnwood, IL: National Textbook, 1992.

Heilenman, Kathy L., Isabelle Kaplan, and Claude Toussaint Tournier. *Voilà: An Introduction to French*. Boston: Heinle & Heinle, 1992.

Higgs, Theodore V. *Teaching for Proficiency: The Organizing Principle*. The ACTFL Foreign Language Education Series. Lincolnwood, IL: National Textbook, 1984.

Jarvis, Gilbert A., Thérèse M. Bonin, and Diane W. Birckbichler. *Invitation: Contextes, culture et communication*. Fort Worth: Holt, Rinehart and Winston, 1993.

Jian, Gérard and Ralph Hester. *Découverte et création: Les bases du français moderne*. Boston: Houghton Mifflin, 1990.

Kramsch, Claire J. "The Cultural Discourse of Foreign Language Textbooks," 63-88 in Alan J. Singerman, ed., *Toward a New Integration of Language and Culture*. Northeast ConferenceReports. Middlebury, VT: Northeast Conference Reports, 1988.

Kulick, Katherine M. and M. Clare Mather. "Culture: Cooperative Learning in the Second-Year Foreign Language Curriculum." *French Review* 66 (1993): 900-7.

Lafayette, Robert C. "Integrating the Teaching of Culture into the Foreign Language Classroom," 47-62 in Alan J. Singerman, ed., *Toward a New Integration of Language and Culture*. Northeast Conference Reports. Middlebury, VT: Northeast Conference Reports, 1988.

Muyskens, Judith A., Alice Omaggio Hadley, and Claudine Convert-Chalmers. *Rendez-vous: An Invitation to French*. New York: McGraw-Hill, 1990.

Oates, Michael D., Larbi Oukada, and Rick Altman. *Entre-Amis: An Interactive Approach to First-Year French*. Boston: Houghton Mifflin, 1991.

Olson, D.R. "On the Language and Authority of Textbooks." *Journal of Communication* 30 (1980): 186-96.

Omaggio, Alice C., ed. *Proficiency, Curriculum, Articulation: The Ties that Bind*. Northeast Conference Reports. Middlebury, VT: Northeast Conference Reports, 1985.

Rosenthal, Alan, Marie de Verneil, and Claude DuVerlie. *Objectif France: Introduction to French and the Francophone World*. Boston: Heinle & Heinle, 1993.

Sanberg, Karl C., Georges Zask, Anthony A. Ciccone, and Françoise Defrecheux. *Ça Marche: Cours de français communicatif.* New York: Macmillan, 1990.

Seelye, H. Ned. *Strategies for Intercultural Communication.* Lincolnwood, IL: National Textbook Company, 1984.

Siskin, H. Jay and Jo Ann M. Recker. *Situations et contextes.* Fort Worth: Holt, Rinehart and Winston, 1990.

Singerman, Alan J. *Toward a New Integration of Language and Culture,* Northeast Conference Reports. Middlebury, VT: Northeast Conference Reports, 1988.

Terrell, Tracy D., Mary B. Rogers, Betsy K. Barnes, and Marguerite Wolff-Hessini. *Deux Mondes: A Communicative Approach.* New York: McGraw-Hill, 1993.

Valette, Jean-Paul and Rebecca Valette. *Contacts: Langue et culture françaises.* Boston: Houghton Mifflin, 1993.

Walz, Joel and Jean-Pierre Piriou. *Rapports: Language, Culture, Communication.* Lexington, MA: D.C. Heath, 1993.

Wood, Hadley, Thomas J. Cox, and Françoise Demerson-Baker. *En Avant: Introduction à la langue et la culture françaises.* Boston: Houghton Mifflin, 1992.

Appendix

Allons-y (Bragger and Rice)	= Textbook A
Voilà (Heilenman, Kaplan, and Tournier)	= Textbook B
Invitation (Jarvis, Bonin, and Birckbichler)	= Textbook C
Découverte et Création (Jian and Hester)	= Textbook D
Rendez-vous (Muyskens, Omaggio, and Convert-Chalmers)	= Textbook E
Entre-Amis (Oates, Oukada, and Altman)	= Textbook F
Objectif France (Rosenthal, De Verneil, and DuVerlie)	= Textbook G
Ça Marche (Sanberg, Zask, Ciccone, and Defrecheux)	= Textbook H
Situations et Contextes (Siskin and Recker)	= Textbook I
Deux Mondes (Terrell, Rogers, Barnes, and Wolff-Hessini)	= Textbook J
Contacts (Valette and Valette)	= Textbook K
Rapports (Walz and Piriou)	= Textbook L
En Avant (Wood, Cox, and Demerson-Baker)	= Textbook M

5
Learning Styles, Personality, and the Foreign Language Teacher

Audrey L. Heining-Boynton
University of North Carolina at Chapel Hill

David B. Heining-Boynton
Meredith College

It has been nearly twenty years since the idea of learning styles became widely recognized on the educational scene. Interest was strong at the time with teachers concerned about the learning styles of their students and how they could best meet their needs. Most of this excitement took place at the beginning of a school year when some school districts administered learning style inventories to all of their students at the start of the school year so that teachers could tailor instruction to meet student needs. At teacher training institutions, learning styles became an integral component of methodology classes across all content areas.

What is interesting is that hundreds of articles have been written on learning styles. Nevertheless, over the course of the past two decades, journals have published a relatively small number of articles about learning styles in the foreign language classroom.

Also unreported are the types of learning styles that foreign language educators exhibit, what types of teaching do they exhibit, and if there is a correlation between the two. Additionally, there are few solid definitions of what exactly is "teaching style."

Gregorc (1979) defines learning styles as "consisting of distinctive behaviors which serve as indicators of how a person learns from and adapts to his environment. It also gives clues as to how a person's mind operates" (234). Most other interpretation of learning styles use a similar definition. However, authors of articles on teaching styles, including Cano (1992), Cornett (1993), Stensrud and Stensrud (1983), and Dunn and Dunn (1979) define teaching styles by example rather than by a specific and universal definition. This suggests that teaching style has something to do with the way one approaches or organizes one's approach to thinking, or how one perceives the learner. Some authors use "style" and "method" inter- changeably, others separate the two. In this paper "teaching style" will be used to describe the focus or approach that the teacher uses to understand information, and in which they are most comfortable using information. These authors suggest, therefore, that there is an important relationship between the learning style of individuals and their teaching style.

Another very popular and important component to describing the learner has been the use of personality type indicators. Upon discerning the personality type of the learner, studies suggest that the teacher can make modifications in the instructional delivery to assist the student in the learning process (Dunn and Dunn, 1979; Cornett, 1983; Henson and Borthwick, 1984). Limited data exist regarding the personality types of foreign language learners, and, as with learning styles, the personality types of foreign language educators have gone unexplored. Are there personality types that typify foreign language teachers? Is there a type that predominates in our profession? Are some personality types more likely to become foreign language educators than others?

The purpose of this paper is to report the findings of an ongoing study that has documented the learning styles as well as the personality types of nearly 100 foreign language teachers. The study sought to answer the following research questions:

- Is there a predominant learning/teaching style among foreign language educators?

- Is there a predominant personality type among foreign language educators?

- What implications do these typings have for foreign language students?

This paper begins with a brief overview of learning styles and personality type indicators. The next section presents a description of the study and an analysis of its results. Finally, the authors explore the implications these results hold for foreign language teaching.

Overview of Learning Style Inventories

Over the decades, numerous learning style inventories have been developed, each with its strengths and limitations. DeBello (1990) compared eleven major learning style models, reporting among other items, the validity of the instrumentation and the research behind the instruments. All of the instrument developers seem to agree on is that learning styles need to be addressed in the curriculum (Spaulding, 1978; Dunn and Dunn, 1979; Cornett, 1983). What is not agreed upon is whether to teach exclusively within the learner's domain, or require them to work outside their preferred learning type.

There is overlap among a number of the theorists' proposed descriptions of learning style types; several divide learning styles into four groups. For example, Kolb (1976) described learners using four different categories: **convergers, divergers, assimilators,** and **accommodators**.

Convergers are known for abstract conceptualization and active experimentation. They excel in the practical application of ideas. **Divergers** are the opposites of convergers. Their strengths lie in their ability for reflective observation and concrete experiences. They have a highly developed ability to imagine the possibilities and are able to view concrete situations from many perspectives. **Assimilators** prefer to employ abstract conceptualization and reflective observation. Creating theoretical models is their forte. Finally, **accommodators** are concrete experiential, and they prefer active experimentation. Accommodators involve themselves in new experiences and prefer to carry out plans and experiments.

McCarthy (1989), who bases her instructional plan on Kolb's Learning Style Inventory (LSI), describes her four learning types:

- **innovative** (curious, aware, and perceptive),
- **analytic** (critical, fact seeking, and philosophizing),
- **common sense** (hands-on, practical, and oriented toward the present),
- **dynamic** (risk taking, adaptive, inventive and enthusiastic).

McCarthy takes her learning inventory a step further by creating a system for teaching. She has developed a method for creating lesson plans that offers all learners the opportunity to be taught 25% of the time in their preferred learning mode, and 75% of the time the learner is challenged by the other three learning types. McCarthy's teaching model affords all students the same pattern of instruction for exactly the same amount of time.

Overview of Personality Type Indicators

Of the personality type instruments available, the Myers-Briggs Type Indicator (MBTI) is extremely popular among educators. For example, researchers like Cano (1992) used the MBTI to assess learning and teaching styles of preservice teachers in agricultural education. In addition to the MBTI, Bargar and Hoover (1984) offered Jung's work on psychological type as a useful guide to studying the teacher, student, learning material, and environment, as well as the interrelation between all of these factors. They cited only a few actual research references from unpublished sources, but emphasized the need and value of using this approach.

The MBTI describes people as being either extrovert/introvert, intuitive/sensing, thinking/feeling, or judging/perceiving. What follows is a brief description of each personality type.

Extroverts (E) enjoy variety and action in their jobs. They tend to dislike complicated procedures, and are frequently impatient with long, slow jobs. They often act quickly, and sometimes without thinking. They enjoy having people around, and do not mind interruptions. Extroverts usually communicate freely (Myers, 1980).

Introverts (I) prefer quiet for concentration and are careful with detail. They dislike sweeping statements. They are content to work on long-term projects, and they work happily alone. Introverts prefer to think a lot before they act, sometimes taking so much time reflecting that they never do act on an issue or item. Introverts have some problems communicating with others (Myers, 1980).

Thinking (T) types guard their emotions and have difficulty dealing with other people's feelings. In fact, they may sometimes offend others without knowing it. They enjoy logical order even if it is at the expense of harmony. They need to be treated fairly, and they are able to reprimand individuals when necessary. Thinking types are analytically oriented and tend to be firm-minded (Myers, 1980).

Feeling (F) types tend to be very aware of other people and their feelings; they enjoy pleasing people, even in small ways. They require harmony in their lives, and do not cope well with disagreements or feuds in the office place. Feeling types need occasional praise. They are people oriented and sympathetic toward others. Often they allow their decisions to be influenced by their own or other people's personal likes and desires (Myers, 1980).

Sensing (S) types are patient with routine and details, reaching a conclusion one step at a time. They seldom make errors of fact and tend to be good at precise work. They like an established way of doing things and dislike new problems unless they are able to employ solutions with which they are familiar. Sensing types rarely experience a spurt of inspiration, and when they do, they tend not to trust it (Myers, 1980).

Intuitive (N) types love solving new problems, usually reaching a conclusion quickly. Precision suffers since intuitive types frequently make errors of fact. They work in bursts of energy powered by enthusiasm, with slack periods in between. Intuitive types dislike routine, yet they are patient with complicated situations (Myers, 1980).

Judging (J) types work best when they are able to make lists, and then follow their plan. They like to reach conclusion on projects. Judging types tend to be satisfied once they reach judgment on a situation or person, but they may decide too quickly. Also, judging types dislike interrupting one project for a more urgent one (Myers, 1980).

Perceptive (P) types adapt well to change. They may procrastinate on unpleasant jobs, and start too many projects at once. They are curious and interested in a new slant or idea on a situation, project, or individual. Perceptive types are open to altering a plan, but they may have difficulty making decisions (Briggs-Myers).

Myers suggests that sensing and feeling types (SF), and intuitive and feeling types (NF), are personality type combinations that are found in teachers. For example, SFs focus their attention on facts, and handle situations with a personal warmth. They are sympathetic and friendly, offering practical help and services for people. NFs focus on the possibilities of a situation, also handling situations with personal warmth like the SFs. NFs are enthusiastic and insightful, and understand and communicate well with people. Sensing and thinking types (ST), and intuitive and thinking types (NT) are more analytical and logical. They tend to handle situations with impersonal analysis. Hence, Myers suggestion that the SFs' and the NFs' personalities are more naturally akin to teaching and other service professions. This does not mean that STs and NTs cannot make good teachers. It simply implies that these individuals tend to be more practical and matter of fact.

Research Project Description

The purpose of this study was to discover if there exists a predominant learning/teaching style among foreign language educators. A second purpose was to discover if foreign language teachers exhibit a predominant personality type. A final question to be answered involves the implications that these typings have for foreign language students.

The research was conducted over a two-year period from 1991 to 1993. Two groups of foreign language teachers, one in Michigan and one in North Carolina, participated in the study. The participants received a demographic questionnaire, the Myers Briggs Type Indicator (MBTI), and Kolb's Learning-Style Inventory (LSI). These were scored, with a copy of the results being given to the participants.[1]

Ninety-one individuals took part in the assessment.   Eight were dropped because of unusable data, and two were used only on some calculations because of incomplete information on one part of the data sheets. Subsequently, 81 individuals were used for all analyses, and 83 individuals were used for part of the analysis.

Demographic Findings

As shown in Table 1, the two groups were composed of 78 females and 5 males. This number is somewhat influenced by the inclusion of a number of FLES teachers. A review of foreign language teacher numbers in several school districts and teacher education programs presents similar indications of a disproportionate ratio of females to males, especially at the elementary level.

Table 1.

Sex	N	%
Females	78	94
Males	5	6
Total	83	100

A second question asked individuals to designate primary and secondary school assignments.

Table 2.

Teaching Level	Level 1		Level 2	
	N	%	N	%
Elementary	23	28	4	44
Middle	7	8	4	44
High School	45	54	0	0
College	7	8	1	11
Total	**83**	**100**	**9**	**100**

Twenty-three individuals taught at the elementary level for their primary placement, seven at the middle school level, 45 at the high school level, and seven at the college level. Four of the elementary teachers also taught at the high school level. Three of the middle school teachers taught at the elementary level with one at the high school level. One of the college teachers also taught at the high school level.

The respondents also designated primary and secondary foreign languages taught as seen in Table 3.

Table 3.

Language	Foreign Language 1		Foreign Language 2	
	N	%	N	%
Spanish	65	78	0	0
French	10	12	11	100
German	4	5	0	0
Latin	3	4	0	0
Other	1	1	0	0
Total	**83**	**100**	**11**	**100**

Spanish was the most frequently mentioned language (78%), with French taught by 12%, German by 5%, and Latin by 4% of the respondents. Only one language, listed as "Other," was mentioned as a primary language. French accounted for all of the second foreign languages taught, and the first language for all of these individuals was Spanish.

As shown in Table 4, individuals responded by placing themselves in age group designations.

Table 4.

Age Group	N	%
20-29	18	22
30-39	14	17
40-49	37	45
50-60 +	14	17
Total	**83**	**100**

Eighteen were in the 20-29 year-old bracket, fourteen in the 30-39 group, thirty-seven in the 40-49 group, and fourteen in the 50-60+ group. Therefore, over half of the participants were over 40. This seems to reflect national teaching demographics that indicate a growing young group of teachers, and an even larger group of teachers at middle age and older.

Members of the groups were also asked to indicate the current educational degree held. (Only two people had less than a bachelor's degree; 44 held a bachelor's degree, 33 a master's degree, and four a doctorate.

Table 5.

Degree Held	N	%
None	1	1
AA	1	1
BA	44	53
MA	33	40
PhD	4	5
Total	**83**	**100**

Results of the MBTI and LSI Assessment

Each participant in the study completed a short form of the MBTI and the LSI. After the instruments were scored, chi-squares were run on the MBTI and LSI information, as well as percentages. Numbers and percentages for a comparison between the MBTI and the LSI can be found in Table 6.

Table 6.

MBTI	LSI-1	LSI-2	LSI-3	LSI-4	SUM-LSI	%
ENFJ		1	1	3	5	6
ENFP	2	2		7	11	14
ENTJ	1	1	1		3	4
ESSJ	6	3	1	10	20	25
ESFP	1	4	1	1	7	9
ESTJ	1	2		1	4	5
ESTP			1		1	1
INFJ	1	3	1	1	6	7
INFP	1	2	1		4	5
INTJ	1				1	1
INTP		1			1	1
ISFJ	2	5			7	9
ISFP	2			2	4	5
ISTJ		5	2		7	9
N =	18	29	9	25	81	
%	22	36	11	31		100

A significant interaction was found between learning styles and personality types ($p = 0.042$). Several other significant factors were noted. One was that LSI-3 (Common Sense or Converger learners) type individuals represented only about 11 percent of the sample. (p< 0.01) Another interesting observation was that three MBTI types were found to be only one LSI type (ESTP, INTJ, INTP), and two MBTI types (ENTP and ISTP) were not represented by any of the 83 subjects (See Table 6). On the other hand, 25% of the entire study population were ESFJ on the Myers Briggs Type Indicator (p< 0.025). This group was represented primarily by learning styles LSI-4, the Dynamic or Accommodator type learner (50%), or LSI-1, the Innovative or Diverger type learner (30%). Another important finding was that MBTI type ENFP included 14% of the individuals (p< 0.02).

Another way of looking at the data was to examine the suggestion by Isabel Briggs Myers (1980) that Sensing and Feeling types (SF) and Intuition and Feeling types (NF) are both likely to be found in the teaching profession. Analysis of the information found in Table 7 indicated a significant difference between Feeling types (78%) and Thinking types (22%) (p< 0.001).

Table 7.

Feeling Types	N	Thinking Types	N
SF	39	NT	5
NF	26	ST	13
Total	**78%**	**Total**	**22%**

This information suggests that individuals who handle situations with personal warmth (while focusing their attention on either facts or possibilities) are more likely to be found in foreign language education than those who are more comfortable with impersonal analysis. Table 7 and the analysis of this data reflect Myers' finding that there is a relationship between SF and NF types and teaching (Myers, 1980), and extend these findings to foreign language educators. Only five of the individuals surveyed interact with their world in a predominantly logical and impersonal way, with a focus on theoretical and technical development. Only 13 of the 83 individuals are focused on technical facts. Instead, 78% of the group seemed to reflect a focus on communicating, understanding, and helping people.

Discussion of the Results

When further reviewing the findings, several interesting facts come to light. One is that only 11% of the subjects were LSI Type Three learners. Among other qualities of Type Threes (Common Sense or Converger learners), these individuals gather data by kinesthetic, hand-on experiences. Since foreign language teaching has not traditionally been involved in this type of learning, our profession may have lost potentially fine teachers because as learners, their needs were not met in the foreign language class. Perhaps now that foreign language has become a more hands-on experience, especially at the elementary school level with foreign language in the elementary school (FLES), we will be seeing more Type Three learners become foreign language educators.

Another statistically significant result is that 25% of the study population are ESFJ on the Myers-Briggs Type Indicator ($p < 0.025$). A description of ESFJ reveals that they are warm-hearted, talkative, popular, conscientious, born cooperators, and active committee members. According to Briggs' description, they are always doing something nice for someone. Among other characteristics, their main interest is in things that directly and visibly affect people's lives. These characteristics strongly describe someone in a service profession such as teaching. Teaching lends itself well to satisfying the needs and personality of ESFJ individuals. Also, they possess the SF combination that Myers suggests is dominant in teachers, and that was discussed earlier in this paper.

It is also interesting to note that no one in the study was an ENTP or an ISTP. Myers describes ENTPs as quick and ingenious who may neglect routine assignments. They turn from one new interest to another. ISTPs are cool onlookers who are quiet and reserved. They analyze life with a detached curiosity. They exert themselves no more than they think necessary, because any waste of energy would be inefficient. Although these two types probably exist as foreign language educators in the entire population of teachers, the characteristics just described would make teaching less than an ideal job for them, in light of the job description of a foreign language teacher.

Finally, no significant interactions were found between age, years taught, level of graduate education, or language taught, and the learning styles and MBTI types. As this data pool grows, it is possible differences between these groups will appear.

Conclusions

The purpose of this study was to discover:

- if there exists a predominant learning/teaching style among foreign language educators;
- if there exists a predominant personality type among foreign language educators;
- what implications this has for foreign language students.

The results of this study show there is no one statistically significant learning/teaching style among foreign language educators. This finding has strong implications for the students of foreign languages. This study suggests that if we support the notion that foreign languages are for everyone, then the types of teachers we are attracting to the profession need to reflect a cross section of the population as well.

Also, the results of the study support the findings by other researchers that certain personality types on the Myers-Briggs Type Indicator are frequently found in the teaching profession. For example, there were a significant proportion of Feeling types over Thinking types in this study population. This is consistent with earlier research on the subject in content areas other than foreign language. This also serves to emphasize the strong relationship between foreign language educators and other teachers. Further, we now have evidence to suggest predominant personality types among foreign language educators. At the same time, foreign language teachers were found to have a diversity of types and styles, demonstrating that individuals with a wide variety of preferences exist in and diversify the profession. As other researchers have suggested, it is important to remember that educators must use a variety of styles—not just their own— to reach all their students (Cornett, 1983; Dunn and Dunn, 1979; Henson and Borthwick, 1984).

Other suggestions for further research include: (1) utilization of the above methodology with a larger sample from multiple national areas, (2) the relationship between types, styles, and successfulness as a foreign language teacher, and (3) trends in students entering the field.

Note

1. The data are also being gathered for a further study comparing trends in foreign language education majors to students majoring in other subjects.

References

Bargar, Robert R. and Hoover, Randy L. "Psychological Type and the Matching of Cognitive Styles." *Theory Into Practice* 23, i (1984): 56-63.

Cano, Jamie. "Learning Styles, Teaching Styles and Personality Styles of Preservice Teachers of Agricultural Education." *Journal of Agricultural Education* 33, i (1992): 46-52.

Cornett, Claudia E. *What You Should Know About Teaching and Learning Styles.* Fastback 191. Bloomington, IN: Phi Delta Kappa Educational Foundation, 1983.

DeBello, Thomas C. "Comparison of Eleven Major Learning Styles Models: Variables, Appropriate Populations, Validity of Instrumentation, and the Research Behind Them." *Reading, Writing, and Learning Disabilities* 6 (1990): 203-222.

Dunn, Rita S. and Dunn, Kenneth J. "Leadership Styles/Teaching styles: Should they...can they...be matched?" *Educational Leadership* 36, iv (1979): 238-44.

Gregorc, Anthony F. "Learning/Teaching Styles: Potent Forces." *Educational Leadership* 36, iv (1979): 234-236.

Henson, Kenneth and Borthwick, Paul. "Matching Styles: A Historical Look." *Theory Into Practice* 23, i (1984): 3-9.

Myers, Isabel Briggs. *Introduction to Type.* Palo Alto, CA: Consulting Psychologists Press, Inc., 1980.

Kolb, David. *Learning Style Inventory: Technical Manual.* Boston, MA: McBer, 1976.

McCarthy, Bernice. *The 4MAT System: Teaching to Learning Styles with Right/Left Mode Techniques.* Barrington, IL: Excel, 1989.

Spaulding, Robert L. "Adapting Teaching Styles to Learning Styles." *Journal of Classroom Interaction* 14, i (1978): 10-18.

Stensrud, Robert and Stensrud, Kay. "Teaching Styles and Learning Styles of Public School Teachers." *Perceptual and Motor Skills* 56, ii (1993): 414.

6

Other Voices: Afro-Hispanic and Francophone Literature

David C. Alley
Clara Krug
Georgia Southern University

A group of white and black students, when asked to identify some of the European ethnic groups that settled in the United States, quickly name the Irish, French, Dutch, German, Italian, and Portuguese. The same students, when asked to identify ethnic groups from the African-American population, struggle to name more than one (Asante, 21).

Until recently American students knew little of the history and contributions of African-Americans despite their presence on the North American continent for almost 400 years. While white students routinely learned about their European heritage, black students were victims of a simple truth of the American educational system: the more they studied, the less they knew about their own culture. This phenomenon was due to an academic canon that systematically focused on the accomplishments of Europeans while ignoring those of other ethnic groups. For example, a survey of popular literary anthologies used in high schools found an exceedingly narrow sampling of African-American writing. The characters in the few African-American works included in these anthologies were largely one-dimensional, distinguished more by their status as victims than their individuality (Pace, 35-36).

In recent years there has been an increased attempt to teach the history of Africa and to explain the unique circumstances that brought Africans to the Americas. This new orientation affirms the value of the African-American heritage by allowing black students to see their ancestors as real people, not just as by-products of the European experience. It also attempts to teach all students the values of tolerance and respect for diversity.

At first glance it would seem that this debate would have little relevance to the teaching of foreign languages. After all, does foreign language instruction by its very nature not instill principles of tolerance and respect for cultural diversity? The answer is not always an unequivocal "yes," however. Cultural instruction often takes a back seat to the teaching of the grammar and vocabulary of the foreign language. Even when cultural information is included as part of the curriculum, that curriculum may omit information related to minority groups within the foreign culture. Students receive only a partial view of the target language culture similar to the exclusively eurocentric view prevalent in other disciplines.

The teaching of French provides a useful example. For decades, the study of French culture has been within an exclusively European context, but information about francophone Africa has received only cursory attention. Moreover, when teachers include African topics, their presentation often tends to reinforce rather than dispel prevailing stereotypes. Mamadou Gueye summarizes his survey of high school textbooks by saying, "The information on Africa is such that the French speaking nations in Africa seem to be culturally inferior to France or the western world in general" (quoted in Mortimer, "Review of L'Afrique," 515). In general, college textbooks have followed suit. There are exceptions. In the first-year textbook *La Clef des champs* (Geoffroy), the central characters are a francophone French-African family in which both parents have professions outside the home. In the preface to the second edition of the second-year reader *Nouveau visage du monde français*, the authors highlight a philosophical change represented in the book: "Since [the first edition], we have all learned to understand and, in some cases, to accept that France is no longer a museum country where we take students on summer courses, that French Canadians use another name, that Africa is making its claim to our modern way of life" (Curcio et al., vi).

This not so benign neglect of francophone Africa extends to textbooks designed for upper-level classes. As Bruner points out, "Despite the size of our universities and the proliferation of courses of current and relevant interest, francophone African literature is still largely unknown" (862). However, both the number and cultural vitality of these non-European French speakers make the exclusion of francophone African culture and literature difficult to justify. As Haig argues, "...the literary productions of Africa, the Caribbean and Québec are no longer to be classed as *'connexes et marginales'* (to those of the hexagon)" (723). Unfortunately, American textbook companies have not typically cooperated by publishing on a long-term basis literary anthologies dedicated to texts from Africa and the Antilles. For example, neither *Contes africains* (Mortimer) nor *Palabres* (Harris), anthologies of francophone texts which students at various proficiency levels enjoy, remains in print. The former has been out-of-print since the late 1980's and the latter since the mid 1980's. Only one general literary anthology, *Littérature francophone* (Joubert), includes texts from Africa along with those from Europe, Canada, the Caribbean, and Southeast Asia. It is published in France. This dearth of readily available texts has kept American teachers hard pressed to identify and procure francophone African texts suitable for the proficiency levels of their students.

Beginning Spanish textbooks and literary anthologies have also overlooked both the contemporary African presence in Latin America and the role Africans have played in the history of the Spanish-speaking peoples. Only in recent years have they paid attention to the diverse racial background of Latin America. The following is a brief but rare example of information related to Afro-Hispanics from a college-level text: "Las personas de habla española representan una población muy diversa: de orígen español, indio, mestizo, negro e inmigrantes europeos de varios países" [Spanish-speaking people represent a very diverse population: Spanish, Indian, mestizo, black and European immigrants from various countries] (Dawson, 29). Advanced-level anthologies also typically include few if any Afro-Hispanic writers.

Publishers often use the minority status of Afro-Hispanics to justify their exclusion from textbooks and anthologies, yet this justification ignores several important facts. First, a great deal of available demographic data is suspect since many Latin American countries fail to compile information concerning their black minorities. Rout, for example, describes a census in Colombia in which the entire black and mulatto populations of two departments went unreported in an apparent attempt to minimize undesirable data (243).

Secondly, although exact numbers are debatable, Afro-Hispanics undeniably represent a rapidly growing population in a significant number of Latin American countries including Colombia, Cuba, the Dominican Republic, Panama, Venezuela, Ecuador, and Nicaragua (Kennedy,

Relatos, ix). Even in those countries where the Afro-Hispanic population is verifiably small, the contribution of this group to the culture at large is disproportionately significant. Examples of this phenomenon appear in tourist brochures of many Latin American countries which, despite their small black populations, focus on Afro-Hispanic cultural contributions such as dance, music, and festivals.

Neither minority status nor questions concerning literary value justify the exclusion of Afro-Hispanic and francophone culture from the foreign language curriculum. To overlook these ethnic groups is to ignore fascinating questions concerning non-Western cultures, the diaspora, the struggle for equality, the preservation of cultural traditions, and contemporary racial relations. The inclusion of Afro-Hispanic and francophone culture is of interest to all foreign language students but it is particularly relevant to black students who have traditionally either avoided foreign language study or dropped out after a short, unsuccessful experience. Only three studies over the last 50 years have addressed this issue, but all three concluded that African-Americans generally do not perform as well as members of other ethnic groups in the study of foreign languages (Davis, "African-American Students," 3). Hancock believes that African-Americans have difficulty because foreign language teachers expect them to straddle too many cultures at the same time. One of those cultures is that of the white European on which textbooks often focus. As a solution he advocates that "African-based content must enter the American school curriculum at all levels" (Hancock). When it does, African-American students will feel as if teachers and the curriculum are including them, not attempting to assimilate them.

In a survey of African-American students, Canto-Lugo and Reich recorded a series of comments regarding attitudes toward foreign language. Two examples of these comments were: "My English is not good enough to learn a foreign language," and "When I took French in my senior year of high school, I found that the teacher was hostile towards my accent. Since then I don't really care for foreign languages" (139). Kennedy claims that one of the reasons for high attrition among black students in foreign language classes is that quite often these students feel little affinity with the traditional cultural content of the courses ("Strategies," 679). Davis and Markham reinforce this point of view, citing a survey that found that 40% of black students believe that their foreign language classes would be more relevant to them if African themes received greater emphasis in first and second year courses (234). Not only black students would benefit from the inclusion of Afro-Hispanic and francophone themes. American students of foreign languages often conceive of the foreign culture as uniform and monolithic. Providing information about minority cultures enables all students to make comparisons and contrasts with their own culture and to deepen their understanding of issues of diversity and tolerance.

Prereading activities

If we accept the need for greater attention to Afro-Hispanic and francophone themes within the foreign language class, we must consider the practical questions related to identifying appropriate techniques for teaching culture, developing new instructional materials and integrating these materials into the existing curriculum. In terms of appropriate methodology, Davis cautions against rote memorization of cultural and historical data, asserting that such a methodology may further enhance students' preconceived negative stereotypes ("Approaches," 28). Tuttle et al. report a comparable negative impact when students are introduced to cultural differences before cultural similiarities (178). A more appropriate methodology for the teaching of culture would assign tasks that trigger an awareness in students of culturally conditioned modes of behavior. An example of an introductory cultural lesson is provided by Mantle-Bromley (122). In this lesson the teacher presents ten examples of American culture-bound behavior (driving on the right-side of the road) and ten examples of individual behaviors (you prefer to shower in the morning). The teacher then divides the chalkboard into two halves labeled YES and NO and asks the students to assign the previously prepared behaviors to one of the two columns. By using this type of inductive approach, students actively participate in forming a working definition of American culture.

A similar activity that would serve to introduce African cultural themes to a French class would be to write the following question on the chalkboard: "Quand vous entendez ou voyez le mot 'Afrique,' à quoi pensez-vous?" (When you hear or see the word "Africa," what do you think of?) After five minutes, the teacher, serving as class secretary, writes student answers on the chalkboard. Students explain the meaning of words that classmates do not understand. One student makes a copy of the list of responses for the teacher. Typical items included on students' lists are: *utilisée par les Européens, une grande population d'indigènes, un climat chaud et humide, beaucoup de pauvreté, l'apartheïd, la jungle, commencement de l'histoire humaine, des animaux, une culture différente,l'art, une vie plus simple.* The culminating activity of the unit or course might be repetition of the same activity. Responses tend to focus on specifics rather than on the generalizations that dominate the earlier list. Typical items are: *une variété de langues—baoulé, malinké, peul, soussou, moré, arabe; des religions différentes—l'Islam, le christianisme, l'animisme; un contraste entre la vie traditionnelle et la vie moderne; les rôles de la femme; les empires anciens—le Mossi, le Ghana, le Mali; l'outrage à cause de la colonisation.*

Another technique that taps into pre-existing cultural knowledge is to present students with a series of statements and ask them to decide whether they are true or false. An example that presents aspects of Afro-Hispanic culture as well as North American culture is found below.

CUESTIONARIO
(Questionnaire)

¿Verdad o falso? (True or false?)

1. _____ *El prejucio racial no existe en América Latina.* (Racial prejudice doesn't exist in Latin America.)

2. _____ *En algunos paises latinoamericanos casi 50% de la población es de ascendencia africana.* (In some Latin American countries, almost 50% of the population is of African heritage.)

3. _____ *Es raro que un hombre negro se case con una mujer blanca en los Estados Unidos.* (It is rare that a black man marries a white woman in the United States.)

4. _____ *Es raro que un hombre negro se case con una mujer blanca en América Latina.* (It is rare that a black man marries a white woman in Latin America.)

5. _____ *En los Estados Unidos la discriminación se basa en los factores raciales; en América Latina se basa en factores económicos.* (In the United States discrimination is based on racial factors; in Latin America it is based on economic factors.)

Since many of the statements are controversial and do not have clear-cut answers, the ensuing discussion is a valuable exercise for introducing Afro-Hispanic culture and contrasting it with the culture of Afro-Americans in the United States.

Instructional materials

In addition to an active, student-centered methodology, we must also pay attention to the development of instructional materials that capture student interest while avoiding oversimplification of complex cultural phenomena. Several writers (Lalande, Purcell, Kramsch) have advocated the use of literary texts as examples of authentic cultural behavior. However, much of the readily available francophone and afro-hispanic literature poses special problems for the beginning and intermediate language student. For example, in a poem, concepts or ideas related to the foreign culture may be represented by certain vocabulary items that are difficult for students to understand. Understanding them may be crucial to comprehension of the theme. Even when they understand vocabulary and imagery, students may find it difficult to identify with some themes; they may also find it difficult to identify with certain morals presented in short stories. Anthologies may include samples of authentic texts designed for a proficiency level beyond that of the students. We must, therefore, select texts which are accessible to our students so that they will be able to learn more readily about francophone and Afro-Hispanic cultures.

A successful technique for studying a variety of genres is one devised by Janet Swaffar and Katherine Arens of the University of Texas at Austin. Their "cognitive process" approach is based on eight fundamental assumptions. Three are especially important:

1) Authentic texts are preferable because the natural linguistic redundancies and language contexts in them aid readers.

2) Adult language learners need to read materials oriented toward adults.

3) One should teach in the target language, relying on inferencing and logical strategies which the adult learner has in his or her native language (Swaffar, 2).

As a result of these assumptions, Swaffar and Arens devised a reading sheet to help adult learners approach and understand authentic texts written in a foreign language. It is designed to help students distinguish between skimming and reading for detail. In addition, to help them as they read for detail, the exercises include tasks whose degree of difficulty increases according to the order of Benjamin Bloom's taxonomy of the cognitive domain: knowledge, comprehension, application, analysis/ synthesis, and evaluation (Bloom, 271-273).

Before reading a text for detail, during class, students skim it for five minutes and then write the main idea in the target language. Several student volunteers write their main-idea sentences on the chalkboard for analysis. All students evaluate the accuracy of content in the responses. Then they correct any spelling and grammar mistakes. The goal of this initial contact is to steer everyone in the right direction. Overnight, students read the text and complete the cognitive process reading sheet. Exercises on that sheet begin at the knowledge and comprehension level of the cognitive domain: making lists of the people, plants, and animals in the text; making a list of the words that make students think of Africa, the Antilles, or Latin America; describing the setting, etc. They advance to the analysis or synthesis level: identifying causes of changes in the setting or the lifestyle of a character; explaining differences in the way that supernatural forces treat a character.

Finally, students must advance to the highest stage of the cognitive domain—evaluation. For example, they may need to imagine why an ethnic group invented a certain legend or guess which natural phenomenon a story or poem describes. The following day, as class begins, volunteers write their answers to knowledge/comprehension level and analysis/synthesis level exercises on the chalkboard. Other students add items to these lists and correct grammatical errors in them. During discussion of these responses, students make additional corrections and revisions. Finally, students read and discuss their answers to the evaluation level questions. The teacher serves as an orchestrator, providing corrections only at the end of class discussion. If there are egregious problems in comprehension, the teacher refers students to the text and helps them discover information that they missed in their earlier close study. All writing and discussion are in the target language. A legend from the Ivory Coast, and a folktale from Latin America, and cognitive process reading sheets to accompany them are included in appendices One and Two.

Like legends and folk tales, poetry is another rich source of material for the study of francophone and afro-hispanic culture. As mentioned previously, faculty need to take care in selecting individual poems. In addition to concerns related to vocabulary and theme, selecting poems necessitates consideration of length, form and stylistic devices. A poem should not be so long that it loses the students hopelessly before it ends. However, it should not be so short as to be hermetic; an elementary or intermediate student might be hopelessly confused. A stanzaic form helps students search for ideas from one stanza to another much as they do from one paragraph to another in a prose text. Then they compare ideas in one stanza with those in another looking for either continuity or discord. Finally, the stylistic device of repetition sometimes helps students realize which elements of a poem are most important. That repetition may take the form of individual vocabulary or of a refrain.

Once teachers have selected individual poems, they need to carefully arrange the sequence in which they present the poems to students, from the easiest to the greatest level of difficulty. Two examples of francophone and afro-hispanic poetry are found in appendices Three and Four. The first is "Celui qui a tout perdu" by David Diop, a Camerounian. The exotic vocabulary is actually minimal, and students understand it easily: *crocodiles, nos danses, le rythme frénétique, le tam-tam, leur nudité, l'esclavage.* The theme is outrage at enslavement. The poem has twenty verses divided into stanzas of equal length. One stanza presents life before enslavement; the other presents life afterward. The repetition of the word "tam-tam" is important in both stanzas.

The second poem is by the Puerto Rican writer Luis Palés Matos. Like the French poem, many of the references to specific countries and animals are easily undertood. The poem is also quite rhythmic with a great deal of repetition and frequent use of onomatopoeic words. The theme deals with the indomitable spirit of Africa which manifests itself in the music and the dance of Africans all over the world.

In addition to traditional narratives and poems, there are a number of films that vividly recreate francophone and Afro-Hispanic themes. The film *Wênd Kûunî* portrays life in Burkina Faso during the Mossi Empire, long before the arrival of white men. As its story unfolds, the film depicts the daily life of men, women, and children in both the countryside and towns. It becomes clear that there is a division of labor between men and women, and that boys and girls are trained at an early age to learn skills appropriate to the tasks that they will be expected to perform as adults. This depiction is a sub-text that the viewer might miss in an effort to follow subtitles and understand the story of the mute boy, Wênd Kûunî. The following guide for taking notes has helped students focus on both daily routine during the Mossi Empire and the singular experience of Wênd Kûunî as they view and discuss the 67-minute film during a two-day period:

Notes au sujet du film "Wênd Kûunî" du Burkina Faso
(Notes on the topic of the film *Wênd Kûnnî* from Burkina Faso)

I.   *Le travail* (Work)

    A. *Des hommes* (Men)

    B. *Des femmes* (Women)

II.   *Des aspects de la vie quotidienne* (Aspects of daily life)

III. *L'intrigue du film = ce qui se passe* (The film's plot = what happens)

IV.   *Votre opinion personnelle* (Your personal opinion)

The format of this guide mirrors that of the cognitive process reading sheet which students have not yet seen. That is, tasks that students complete increase in degree of difficulty from knowledge and comprehension (I and II) to comprehension and analysis (III) and finally to evaluation (IV). Students watch and take notes on the first part of the film on the first day of the course or the unit, just after discussing the lists that they have generated about "Afrique." Viewing and notetaking continue on the second day, and discussion begins. The guide's format also helps students focus on certain aspects of the film that anticipate various literary texts that they may study during a particular course or over a longer period of time. As they read legends, stories, poems, and novels, students use *Wênd Kûunî* as a point of reference for elements of the traditional lifestyle in parts of former French West Africa. For example, the role of women in *Wênd Kûunî* is the same as their role in various short stories and in the autobiography *L'Enfant Noir*. However, it contrasts with the role of Pokou in "La Légende Baoulé" and with that of the newly divorced Ramatoulaye in *Une si longue lettre*. The guide also helps students begin to focus on style. The film is actually a "frame story" that returns to its initial focus during the plot's climax and dénouement, just as "Les Mamelles" returns to its initial focus of two Senegalese mountains, and "Maman Caiman" returns to that of the superior intelligence of alligators.

Another effective method for analyzing films has been developed by Shumaker for use in her course "Latin American Culture Through Film" at Georgia Southern University. After watching a particular film, students are asked to prepare an abstract using the following outline:

Título: *Sitio de acción:*
Año de acción: *Ubicación histórica:*
Personajes principales: *Resumen breve de la trama:*
Tema o temas principales: *Opinión personal:*

This type of abstracting procedure, while allowing for personal reaction, forces students to consider the film in a more objective manner. It also reinforces what Altman refers to as the Golden Rule of Video Pedagogy: full comprehension of the video text is not necessary in order to understand the basic plot and overriding themes (42-43).

Two films that give insight into the history of slavery in Latin America are *El otro Francisco* and *La última cena*. *El otro Francisco* portrays the brutality of slavery in general and the abuses of women slaves in particular. *La última cena* tells the story of a master who attempts to instruct his slaves in the values of Christianity only to discover that religion and slave ownership are incompatible.

Slave rebellions were common throughout Latin America, and two films portray this little-known aspect of slavery in two different countries. The film *Cimarrones* recreates life in a fictional "palenque" community of escaped slaves in 19th century Peru. A documentary entitled *Palenque: Un canto* traces the history of a small Colombian town which was founded by escaped slaves and exists to the present day.

Miscegenation or the blending together of races is also common theme in Afro-Hispanic literature. One film that deals with this controversial topic is *Cecilia* based on the 19th century novel *Cecilia Valdés* by Cirilio Villaverde. Although a great deal of racial mixing did occur throughout Latin America, the film demonstrates the intransigence of a social hierarchy based on skin color.

Significant blending has also occurred in the area of religion when African slaves, who were forced to convert to Christianity, covertly combined their traditional African gods with the new Christian saints. Although this syncretism is common throughout Latin American, two films that deal with this phenomenon were both produced in Brazil: *A Samba da Criação do Mundo* and *O Pagador de Promesas*. A third film, *Bahia: Africa in the Americas*, was a National Geographic special some years ago. All three films are available for loan through the Roger Thayer Stone Center for Latin American Studies at Tulane University. A complete address for the Center can be found in the bibliography.

Conclusion

In her introduction to *Contes africains*, Mildred Mortimer focuses on the unique contribution of the oral tradition of African ethnic groups:

> African culture has too often been minimized by those who equated "oral tradition" with lack of culture. The imprint of colonialism (conquerors deriding the conquered) and linguistic barriers (before bilingual writers and anthropologists brought light to obscurity) have been responsible for a gross simplification of Africa's offerings and attributes (xii-xiii).

Contemporary francophone African writers such as Bernard Dadié have emphasized the unique legends and fables emanating from this oral tradition as an important component of the literature of "négritude." To keep this tradition alive, they have transcribed oral literature from various languages into French. Poets, dramatists, and novelists from former French West Africa, the Antilles, and Latin America have added a corpus of works based on their own experiences. To highlight the importance of being black, black Africans and Afro-Hispanics have added to world literature both traditional and modern texts that have the potential to touch all people. However, in the United States, it is difficult for teachers to incorporate such texts in the curriculum. Some are out-of-print. The proficiency level required to understand others is too advanced for many students. Many teachers and students are unacquainted with the art, history, music, civilization, and politics of areas which produced these texts. Nonetheless, it is incumbent upon teachers of French and Spanish in American high schools, colleges and universities to surmount these obstacles because students of all colors and ethnic groups can benefit from studying such universal texts.

References

Altman, Rick. *The Video Connection: Integrating Video into Language Teaching.* Boston: Houghton Mifflin Company, 1989.

Asante, Molefi Kete. "Learning about Africa." *The Executive Educator* 14 (1992): 21-25.

Bloom, Benjamin S., J. Thomas Hastings, and George F. Madaus. *Handbook on Formative and Summative Evaluation of Student Learning.* New York: McGraw-Hill Book Company, 1971.

Bruner, Charlotte H. "An Audiovisual Presentation of Black Francophone Poetry," *The French Review*, LV, 6 (1982): 862-868.

Canto-Lugo, Ramiro and Matthew J. Reich. "An Initial Investigation Into Why More African-American Students Do Not Take Foreign Language Classes," *Extending the Concept and Practice of Classroom Based Research to California Community Colleges*. ERIC, 1992. ED 348 117.

Curcio, Louis L. et al. *Nouveau Visage du monde français*. 2nd ed. Boston: Houghton Mifflin Company, 1981.

Dadié, Bernard. "La Légende Baoulé." *Contes africains*. Mildred Mortimer, ed. Boston: Houghton Mifflin Company, 1972.

Davis, James J. "Approaches to the Teaching of Afro-Hispanic Culture," *Afro-Hispanic Review*, 5, 1 (1980): 28-30.

_____. *African-American Students and Foreign Language Learning*. ERIC, 1992. ED 345 583.

Davis, James J. and Paul L. Markham. "Student Attitudes Toward Foreign Language Study at Historically and Predominantly Black Institutions," *Foreign Language Annals*, 24, 3 (1991): 227-237.

Dawson, Laila M. and Albert C. Dawson. *Dicho y Hecho: Beginning Spanish*. New York: John Wiley & Sons, 1989.

Diop, David. "Celui qui a tout perdu." *Anthologie de la nouvelle poésie nègre et malgache de la langue francaise*. 2nd edition. Léopold Sédar Senghor. Paris: Presses Universitaires de France, 1992.

Geoffroy, R., D. Lo Cascio, & M. Rivas. *La Clef des Champs*. Paris: Larousse, 1991.

Haig, Stirling. Foreword. *The French Review*, LV, 6 (1982): 723.

Hancock, Charles. "Foreign Language Study at the College Level: The African-American Student." [Paper presented at the ACTFL Convention. San Antonio, Texas, November 1993.]

Harris, Rodney E. et al. *Palabres: Contes et poèmes de l'Afrique noire et les Antilles*. Glenview, IL: Scott, Foresman and Company, 1973.

Joubert, Jean-Louis. *Littérature francophone: anthologie*. Paris: Groupe de la Cité international Création-Diffusion, 1992.

Kennedy, James H. *Relatos latinoamericanos: La herencia africana*. Lincolnwood, IL: National Textbook Company, 1986.

_____. "Strategies for Including Afro-Latin American Culture in the Intermediate Spanish Class," *Hispania* 70 (1987): 679-683.

Kramsch, Claire. "Literary Texts in the Classroom: A Discourse Perspective." *The Modern Language Journal* 69 (1985): 356-66.

Lalande John F. II. "Teaching Literature and Culture in the High School Foreign Language Class." *Foreign Language Annals* 21, 6 (1988): 573-581.

Levy-Konesky, Nancy, Karen Daggett, & Lois Cecsarini. *Fronteras: Literatura y cultura.* Fort Worth: Harcourt Brace, 1992.

Mantle-Bromley, Corinne. "Preparing Students for Meaningful Culture Learning." *Foreign Language Annals* 25, 2 (1992): 117-127.

Mortimer, Mildred. "Review of *L'Afrique en français*" by Severine Arlabosse. *The French Review* 61,3 (1988): 515-516.

Pace, Barbara G. "The Textbook Canon." *English Journal* 81 (1992): 33-38.

Palés Matos, Luis. "Danza negra," *Aproximaciones al estudio de la literatura hispánica*, in Edward H. Friedman, L. Teresa Valdivieso, and Carmelo Virgillo, eds., 2nd edition. New York: McGraw-Hill Publishing Company, 1989.

Purcell, John M. "Cultural Appreciation through Literature." *Foreign Language Annals* 21, 1 (1988): 19-24.

Rout, Leslie B. *The African Experience in Spanish America.* Cambridge: Cambridge University Press, 1976.

Shumaker, Nancy. *Latin American Culture through Film.* Department of Foreign Languages, Georgia Southern University, Statesboro, GA 30460.

Swaffar, Janet. *Learning Research Basis for a Process Approach: Distinguishing Learning Models from Teacher Methods.* Workshop for Development of Foreign Language and Literature Programs. MLA Convention. New York, 27 December 1981.

Roger Thayer Stone Center for Latin American Studies. Tulane University. New Orleans, Louisiana, 70118-5698.

Tuttle, Harry et al. "Effects of Cultural Presentations on Attitudes of Students." *Modern Language Journal* 63 (1979): 177-182.

Wênd Kûunî. Dir. Gaston Kaboré. 1982. Available through California Newsreel, San Francisco, California.

Appendix 1

La Légende Baoulé

Il y a longtemps, très longtemps, vivait au bord d'une lagune calme, une tribu paisible de nos frères. Ses jeunes hommes étaient nombreux, nobles et courageux, ses femmes étaient belles et joyeuses. Et leur reine, la reine Pokou, était la plus belle parmi les plus belles.

Depuis longtemps, très longtemps, la paix était sur eux et les esclaves mêmes, fils des captifs des temps révolus, étaient heureux auprès de leurs heureux maîtres.

Un jour, les ennemis vinrent nombreux comme des magnans. Il fallut quitter les paillotes, les plantations, la lagune poissonneuse, laisser les filets, tout abandonner pour fuir. Ils partirent dans la forêt. Ils laissèrent aux épines leurs pagnes, puis leur chair. Il fallait fuir toujours, sans repos, sans trêve, talonné par l'ennemi féroce.

Et leur reine, la reine Pokou, marchait la dernière, portant au dos son enfant. A leur passage l'hyène ricanait, l'éléphant et le sanglier fuyaient, le chimpanzé grognait et le lion étonné s'écartait du chemin.

Enfin, les broussailles apparurent, puis la savane et les rôniers et, encore une fois, la horde entonna son chant d'exil:

> Mi houn Ano, Mi houn Ano, blâ o
> Ebolo nigué, mo ba gnan min—
> Mon mari Ano, mon mari Ano, viens
> Les génies de la brousse m'emportent.

Harassés, exténués, amaigris, ils arrivèrent sur le soir au bord d'un grand fleuve dont la course se brisait sur d'énormes rochers. Et le fleuve mugissait, les flots montaient jusqu'aux cimes des arbres et retombaient et les fugitifs étaient glacés d'effroi. Consternés, ils se regardaient. Etait-ce là l'Eau qui les faisait vivre naguère, l'Eau, leur grande amie? Il avait fallu qu'un mauvais génie l'excitât contre eux. Et les conquérants devenaient plus proches.

Et, pour la première fois, le sorcier parla: "L'eau est devenue mauvaise, dit-il, et elle ne s'apaisera que quand nous lui aurons donné ce que nous avons de plus cher." Et le chant d'espoir retentit:

> Ebe nin flê nin bâ
> Ebe nikn flâ nin nan
> Ebe nin flê nin dja
> Yapen'sè ni djà wali

Quelqu'un appelle son fils
Quelqu'un appelle sa mère
Quelqu'un appelle son père
Les belles fills se marieront.

Et chacun donna ses bracelets d'or et d'ivoire, et tout ce qu'il avait pu sauver. Mais le sorcier les repoussa et montra le jeune prince, le bébé de six mois: "Voilà, dit-il, ce que nous avons de plus précieux."

Et la mère, effrayée, serra son enfant sur son coeur. Mais la mère était aussi la reine et, droite au bord de l'abîme, elle leva l'enfant souriant au-dessus de sa tête et le lança dans l'eau mugissante.

Alors des hippopotames, d'énormes hippopotames émergèrent et, se plaçant les uns à la suite des autres, formèrent un pont et sur ce pont miraculeux, le peuple en fuite passa en chantant:

Ebe nin flê nin bâ
Ebe nin flê nin nan
Ebe nin flê in dja
Yapen'sè ni djà wali
Quelqu'un appelle son fils
Quelqu'un appelle sa mère
Quelqu'un appelle son frère
Les belles filles se marieront.

Et la reine Pokou passa la dernière et trouva sur la rive son peuple prosterne. Mais la reine était aussi la mère et elle put dire seulement "baouli," ce qui veut dire: l'enfant est mort.

Et c'était la reine Pokou et le peuple garda le nom de Baoulé (Dadié 1-7).

Feuille de lecture pour "La Légende Baoulé"

   I. Premier Contact

      A. Regardez la lecture rapidement (5 minutes).

      B. Quelle est l'idée générale de la lecture? Indiquez dans deux ou trois phrases.

  II. Etude du Détail

      A. Identifiez ces éléments du conte:

        1. Les personnes

        2. Les plantes

    3. Les animaux

    4. D'autres éléments de la nature

B. Discussion

    1. Faites une description de la vie au commencement du conte.

    2. Faites une liste des changements dans cette vie.

    3. Faites une description de la vie à la fin du conte.

C. Cause-effet: Lesquels de ces éléments causent les changements dans la vie dans ce conte? Comment?

D. Interprétation: Selon vous, pourquoi est-ce qu'on a inventé ce conte?

Appendix 2

I. Antes de leer

A. Uno de los temas de este cuento es la comida ideal. ¿Cuál es tu comida favorita? ¿Qué es un plato que Ud. sabe preparar bien?

Una leyenda africana

Hace mucho tiempo Obatalá observó que Orula era muy imaginativo. En más de una ocasión, pensó entregarle el mando del mundo, pero al pensarlo detenidamente no lo hizo porque Orula era demasiado joven para una misión de tanta importancia, a pesar del buen juicio y seriedad de todos sus actos. Un día Obatalá quiso saber si Orula era tan capaz como parecía, y le mandó preparar la mejor comida posible.

Orula escuchó los deseos de Obatalá, y sin responder, fue directamente al mercado cercano con el fin de comprar una lengua de toro. La condimentó y cocinó de una manera tan singular que Obatalá, satisfecho, le preguntó la razón por la cual la lengua era la mejor comida que se podía hacer.

Orula respondió a Obatalá:

— Con la lengua se da "aché," se ponderan las cosas, se proclama la virtud, se exaltan las obras y maneras y también se alaba a los hombres...

Cuando pasó algún tiempo, Obatalá le mandó a Orula preparar otra comida, pero esta vez debía ser la peor comida posible.

Orula volvió al mercado, compró otra lengua de toro, la cocinó y se la presentó a Obatalá. Y cuando Obatalá vio la misma comida le dijo:

— ¡Orula! ¿cómo es posible que al servirme esta comida me confesaras que era la mejor y la presentas ahora como la más mala?

Orula respondió a Obatalá:

— Entonces te dije que era la mejor, pero ahora te digo que es la peor, porque con ella se vende y se pierde a un pueblo, se calumnia a las personas, se destruye su buena reputación y se cometen las más repudiables vilezas...

Obatalá, maravillado de la inteligencia y precocidad de Orula, le dio el mando del mundo (Levy-Konesky 12).

II. Primer Contacto
    A.   Lea la lectura rapidamente (5 minutos)
    B.   ¿Cuál es la idea general de la lectura? Escriba dos o tres frases.

III. Estudio de los Detalles
    A.   Escriba una descripción de los personajes principales del cuento.
    B.   Escriba una descripción del problema o conflicto del cuento.
    C.   ¿Cómo termina el cuento?

IV. Extensión
    A.   ¿Hay cuentos norteamericanos parecidos a este?
    B.   Compare este cuento a "Rumplestilskin." ¿Cuáles son las diferencias y las semejanzas?

Appendix 3

Celui qui a tout perdu

Le soleil brillait dans ma case
Et mes femmes étaient belles et souples
Comme les palmiers sous la brise des soirs.
Mes enfants glissaient sur le grand fleuve
Aux profondeurs de mort
Et mes pirogues luttaient avec les crocodiles.
La lune, maternelle, accompagnait nos danses
Le rythme frénétique et lourd du tam-tam,
Tam-tam de la joie, tam-tam de l'insouciance
    Au milieu des feux de liberté.
Puis un jour, le Silence...
Les rayons du soleil semblèrent s'éteindre

Dans ma case vide de sens.
Mes femmes écrasèrent leurs bouches rougies
Sur les lèvres minces et dures des conquérants
    aux yeux d'acier Et
Mes enfants quittèrent leur nudité paisible
Pour l'uniforme de fer et de sang.
Votre voix s'est éteinte aussi
Les fers de l'esclavage ont déchiré mon coeur
Tams-tams-de mes nuits, tams-tams de mes pères.

(Diop 174)

Feuille de lecture pour "Celui qui a tout perdu"

I. Premier Contact
   A. Regardez la lecture rapidement (5 minutes).
   B. Quelle est l'idee générale de ce texte?

II. Etude de Détail
   A. Dans tout le poème, quels mots de vocabulaire associés à l'Afrique est-ce que le poète emploie?
   B. La description de chaque personne ou chaque chose change dans la deuxième strophe. Faites une liste des changements.
   C.
     1. Trouvez les mots dans la première strophe qui donnent un résumé de la situation que le poète décrit dans cette strophe.
     2. Trouvez les mots dans la deuxième strophe qui donnent un résumé de la situation que le poète décrit dans cette strophe.
   D. Comment est-ce que la vie a changé dans la deuxième strophe?
   E. Interprétation: Qu'est-ce que les tams-tams représentent?

Appendix 4

I. Antes de leer

A. En este poema, el poeta emplea algunos sonidos que los animales hacen. ¿Cuáles son los sonidos que hacen los siguientes animales: el gallo, el perro, el cerdo, el pollito?

Danza negra

Calabó y bambú.
Bambú y calabó.
El Gran Cocoroco dice: tu-cu-tú.
La Gran Cocoroca dice: to-co-tó.
Es el sol de hierro que arde en Tombuctú.
Es la danza negra de Fernando Póo.
El cerdo en el fango gruñe: pru-pru-prú.
El sapo en la chacra sueña: cro-cro-cró.
Calabó y bambú.
Bambú y calabó.
Rompen los junjunes en furiosa ú.
Los gongos trepidan con profunda ó.
Es la raza negra que ondulando va
en el ritmo gordo del mariyandá.
Llegan los butucos a la fiesta ya.
Danza que te danza la negrase da.
Calabó y bambú.
Bambú y calabó.
El Gran Cocoroco dice: tu-cu-tú.
La Gran Cocoroca dice: to-co-tó.
Pasan tierras rojas, islas de betún:
Haití, Martinica, Congo, Camerún;
las papiamentosas antillas del ron
y las patualesas islas del volcán,
que en el grave son
del canto se dan.
Calabó y bambú.
Bambú y calabó.
Es el sol de hierro que arde en Tombuctú.
Es la danza negra de Fernando Póo.

El alma africana que vibrando está.
En el ritmo gordo del mariyandá.
Calabó y bambú.
Bambú y calabó.
El Gran Cocoroco dice: tu-cu-tú.
La Gran Cocoroca dice: to-co-tó. (180)

II. Estudio de los detalles
A. Lea el poema rapidamente (5 minutos).
B. ¿Cuál es la idea general de la lectura? Escriba dos o tres frases.

III. Estudio de los detalles
A. ¿Cuáles animales se menciona en el poema?
B. ¿Cuáles referencicas geográficas hay en el poema?
C. Explique la rima y el ritmo en el poema.

IV. Extensión
A. ¿De dónde vienen sus antepasados? ¿Cuáles tradiciones trajeron a este país?
B. Haga un mapa del mundo para mostrar de dónde son los antepasados de los miembros de la clase.

ADVISORY BOARD OF SPONSORS AND PATRONS
SPONSORS AND PATRONS REPRESENTING INSTITUTIONS
February 1993-February 1994

Andrea J. Allaire
John Austin
Marilyn Bedsworth
Susan J. Blankenship
Herman F. Bostick
Georgia Brown
Olga J. Burtnett
Donna R. Butler
Samuel B. Carleton
Marilyn P. Carpenter
Rosalie M. Cheatham
Shepherd J. Chuites
Kay Clements
Luana F. Coleman
Joanna B. Crane
Bob Daley
Emilie Patton de Luca
Janice Dowd
Greg Duncan
Billie Edmonds
Raúl Fernández
Carine Feyten
E. Wayne Figart
Anne Fountain
T. Bruce Fryer
James S. Gates
Antoinette D. Glenn
Carol P. Goings
Richard A. Goodwyn
Marcia Grimes
Keith A. Guess
Moses Hardin

Audrey L. Heining-Boynton
Paula Heusinkveld
Ann N. Hughes
Rebecca B. Irwin
Susan Joris
Julia S. Key
Richard B. Klein
Horst G. Kurz
Leona B. LeBlanc
Sheri Spaine Long
Thomas W. Lott
Monika Lynch
Daniel A. MacLeay
Vesta F. Manning-Smith
C. T. Markham, III
Dave McAlpine
Terry A. McCoy
Sharon H. McCullough
Dan McElderry
Mary B. McGehee
Paula S. McGuire
Jo Ann McNatt
Marcia Miller
Ivy Mitchell
Karen Mitchell
Joann McFerran Mount
Jackie Moyano-Paracha
Helen G. Newton
Fred H. Nieto
Roger A. Noël
Kathleen M. Olson
Eneida Pugh

Louise Rollefson
Virginia M. Scott
Eleanor G. Sharp
Richard L. Shelburne
Nancy W. Shumaker
Sam L. Slick
Robin C. Snyder
Lissi Spencer
Marcia A. Spielberger
Louise Stanford
Mary E. Stovall

Alice J. Strange
Janene C. Sullivan
Robert M. Terry
Sara Toro
Yvonne H. Tutunjian
Leonarda Vanderwerf
JoAnne S. Wilson
Jerry Phillips Winfield
Dorothy Winkles
Ilza Wood

ADVISORY BOARD OF SPONSORS AND PATRONS
SPONSORS AND PATRONS REPRESENTING INSTITUTIONS
February 1993-February 1994

Alabama Association of Foreign Language Teachers	Pat H. Nix
American Association of Teachers of French	Fred M. Jenkins
AATF, Arkansas Chapter	Glenda Carr and Jane C. Williamson
AATF, Florida Chapter	Pearl Bennett Chiari
AATF, Louisiana Chapter	Patricia Duggar
AATF, South Carolina Chapter	Kristine Little and Diana L. Cook
American Association of Teachers of German	Helene Zimmer-Loew
AATSP, Tennessee Chapter	Juanita Shettlesworth
American Classical League	Richard A. LaFleur
American Society of French Academic Palms	Elie de Comminges
Auburn University	Mary M. Millman and Linda W. Shabo
Belmont University	J.H.E. Paine and Cheryl Brown
Central States Conference on Language Teaching	Jody Thrush
Chipola Junior College	Loletia Henson
Coffee High School, Douglas, GA.	Scott Grubbs and Linda McCullar
College of Charleston	Michael S. Pincus
Daytona Beach Community College	Munir Sarkis & Susan Stewart-Rae
Emory University	Viola G. Westbrook
Florida Foreign Language Association	Aurelia Ogles
Foreign Language Association of Georgia	Liz Bouis
Foreign Language Association of NC	Kathy White and Fran Head
Florida Foreign Language Instructors in Community Colleges	Lillian S. Unger
French Education Project - LSU	Robert C. LaFayette
Fulton County Board of Education	Lynne McClendon
Furman University	C. Maurice Cherry
Georgia Southern University	Judith H. Schomber
Georgia State University	Anna V. Lambros

Kennesaw State College   Elaine McAllister
Lakeside High School, Evans, GA   Jane Shaffer Elliott
Longwood College   Ellery Sedgwick
Louisiana Foreign Language Association   Joan Chardkoff
Macon College   Lynne Bryan and Rosemary Dumas
Middle Tennessee State University   Judith Rusciolelli and
                                                               Dianne Harper
Mississippi Foreign Language Association   Teresa R. Arrington
North Carolina State University   Susan Navey Davis
North Georgia College   W. Guy Oliver
Northeast Conference on Language Teaching   Lisa Holekamp
Pacific Northwest Council on Foreign Languages   Ray Verzasconi
Paulding County Schools, Douglasville, GA   Maureen W. Clouse
                                                            and Judy V. Henry
Porter-Gaud School, Charleston, SC   Allyn S. Bruce
                                                           and Gladys Ingram
Samford University   Myralyn Allgood
Savannah-Chatham County Schools   Donna Meyers
Southwest Conference on Language Teaching   Joanne K. Pompa
Spelman College   Frank Langhorst
University of Montevallo   Michael Rowland and Richard W. Thames
Univeristy of South Florida   Robert W. Cole
University of South Carolina   Carolyn Hansen andArthur Mosher
University of North Carolina - Greensboro   Carmen Sotomayer
University of Mobile   Nancy N. Wall
Valdosta State University   Lee Bradley and Sandra Walker
Virginia Polytechnic & State University   Christopher Eustis
Wheeler High School-Spanish Honor Society   Patricia M. Matias
Winthrop University   Guillermo I. Castillo-Feliu

SCOLT Publications
Valdosta State University
Valdosta, Georgia 31698
☎ **912-333-7358** FAX **912-333-7389**
lbradley@grits.valdosta.peachnet.edu
scolt@catfish.valdosta.peachnet.edu

Order Form

number
of copies

_____ Terry, Robert M., ed. *Changing Images in Foreign Languages; Dimension: Language '94*. (Selected and refereed articles from the Proceedings of the 1994 Annual Conference). Valdosta State University, GA: Southern Conference on Language Teaching, 1994. $10.00 prepaid
ISBN 1-883640-02-4   LCCN 94-67409

_____ Terry, Robert M., ed. *Internationalizing the Future; Dimension: Language '92-'93*. (Selected and refereed articles from the Proceedings of the 1992-1993 Annual Conference). Valdosta State University, GA: Southern Conference on Language Teaching, 1993. $10.00 prepaid
ISBN 1-883640-01-6   LCCN 93-84571

_____ Slick, Sam L., and Richard B. Klein, eds. *Managing the Foreign Language Department: A Chairperson's Primer.* Valdosta State University, GA: Southern Conference on Language Teaching, 1993. $20.00 prepaid
ISBN 1-883640-00-8   LCCN 93-84304

SCOLT is a non-profit 501(c)3 educational organization.
EIN 23-7017288

Name _____

School Address _____

_____

City _____ State _____ Zip _____